INDIA POLARISED

L K SHARMA

factionbooks@gmail.com

Some of these articles were published in
Mainstream, Open Democracy and *The Wire*

CONTENTS

POEMS

One Man, two Communities make a Troubled Nation

India's transformation since 2014, brought about by a self-certified Nonbiological Being (NB), is highlighted by the most-asked question: Is India democratic and secular? It is raised in India and world-wide. Foreign agencies record India's pathetic ranking in the indexes tracking democracy and civil liberties. All ignored by those mesmerised by NB's populist rhetoric, fake religiosity, false promises and '*All-izz-Well*' slogan.

The curse of 2014 will last long. How this story of India's most dangerous decade will conclude remains to be seen. In the sixties, foreign scholars and journalists had wondered whether India would survive. Today, Indians write gloomy books on the failing democracy and religious polarisation. The rise of 'Hindutva' is a new menacing factor. Even in its nascent stage, 'Hindutva' had partnered with the Muslim League to promote the two-nation theory, leading to the partition. But then Indian nationalism overwhelmed Hindu nationalism and India survived. Will India confound its critics again? The officially propagated Hindu nationalism is dangerous. The resurgent 'Hindutva' is accompanied by a vicious hate campaign and violence against Muslims. It poses a graver challenge to Indian nationalism than what the chaotic mass movements had done in the past?

India's current Hindu-Muslim polarisation has revived memories of the biggest tragedy that struck the subcontinent immediately after it got free. The partition in 1947 was a humanitarian crisis seen in grim black-and-white photographs. The brutal events of 1947 struck like thunderbolt, devastating selected sections of people and areas and enveloping all others in a blanket of ethical grey. Today's new mentally divided India is reflected in colourful videos and vicious text running on the mobile screens. Today's divisions have no limits and are part of a sustained polarisation process that affects the whole nation. The partition violence was big and blatant; it precipitated suddenly on an unsuspecting population. Today's psycho-social maneuvers are low-level and insidious. This violence also affects Hinduism and the Idea of India and will have graver repercussions.

The politically driven distortion of Hinduism has made some Hindus disown their faith, sullied the religion's image, and reduced its brand value in the international faith market. The 1947 partition was caused by a clearly marked religious division. Today, every faith tradition and every family is divided because most Hindus disapprove of hatred towards Muslims. Liberal Hindus as well as true believers protest the hijacking of their ancient religion by political operators for electoral gains. Such Hindus actively resist majoritarian and anti-democratic trends. They share the pain of the community that feels besieged and intimidated. I am able to write this because my name is not Khan.

The present religious polarisation did not erupt suddenly. The New Age of Ram began in India with a *Rath Yatra* in 1990, centuries after Lord Ram appeared as an incarnation of Vishnu. BJP leader Lal Krishna Advani started from the holy city of Somnath in Gujarat in an airconditioned Toyota, decorated as a traditional *rath* (chariot seen in mythological movies). Thus the campaign to erect a Ram temple on the site of the 15th-century Babri Masjid was formally launched. It triggered religious violence that took a toll of 2,000 lives. The Hindu right-wing saw the political dividend yielded by polarisation and adopted it as its electoral strategy. Militant religious fervour sparked by the *Rath Yatra* continued and on December 6, 1992, a mob bearing hammers and axes, enthused by the BJP leaders' fiery speeches, demolished the mosque. The triumphant mob and the levelled mosque were televised worldwide.

The 1992 Bombay riots and the 1998 Coimbatore incidents were a trailer of the future to come. Ten years after the mosque demolition, another chapter was written in the Ram saga. In 2002, fifty-nine 'Ram devotees' returning from Ayodhya to Gujarat on the Sabarmati Express were burnt alive in a train in Godhra in Gujarat. Their bodies were paraded in the State. Hindus retaliated and killed Muslims in large numbers. Whether the train arson was a conspiracy or an accident was disputed but the official line holding the Muslims responsible prevailed. Violence against Muslims spread far and wide under the watch of chief minister Narendra Modi and took a toll of another 2,000 lives. Gandhi's Gujarat was transformed. Communal hatred spread among communities and age groups who had not witnessed the 1947 Partition riots. After the demolition of the Babri Mosque, the communal virus appeared in 'those like us'. Unsayable things began to be said at the dining tables. Many, it seemed, wanted a Hindu Aurangzeb to settle scores with the Mughal Emperor who died in 1707. 'Hindu nationalism' and 'Hindu Rashtra' entered serious political discourse. The religious right-wing used history, mythology, and misinformation to promote its ideology. By 2014, the BJP and RSS had made Hindus aware of Aurangzeb's reign. They ignore historical facts about Aurangzeb helping to establish several Hindu temples (like the Someshwar Mahadev temple). Historians say that no religious antipathy was involved in the attacks on the Hindu temples, which were also attacked by victorious Hindu kings like the (Chandelas and Cholas) because of the wealth hidden in them. Such historians are called anti-national.

Wither Scientific Temper

Tagore, Gandhi, and Nehru inspired the people to control hatred and fear and imbibe modernity and rational thinking. Tagore critiqued nationalism.

Influenced by such leaders, the faith-driven people of India learnt to keep religion and politics apart, frustrating for decades the Hindu right-wing who hated secularism and pluralism and Gandhi. Physical signs of fake modernity proliferate as India trudges back towards medievalism. Scientists read ridiculous 'scientific' statements by Modi and other BJP leaders and lament the diminishing scientific temper. Close down all scientific labs, an eminent scientist cries. It is not just ignorance. It is a political Godman's project to bury the Nehruvian India in which masses cheered Nehru when he called development projects 'modern temples'. They heeded Nehru's warnings against blind faith, superstitions and communalism and his drive to inculcate scientific temper. One boasted about the Indian Constitution having a reference to 'scientific temper' and saw India set on the path of modernity and progress by Gandhi, Nehru, and other reformist Hindu leaders. It now appears as a distant past. Of course, even during those years, a communal clash would take place now and then, but its impact would not last. Now one sees sustained low-level violence and toxic social media posts by diseased minds.

The political force responsible for the change gathered momentum after the demolition of the Babri mosque. While in Opposition, the Hindu right-wing used democratically made available civil liberties and free press to popularise the 'Hindu Rashtra'. Its leaders did the groundwork to 'awaken' Hindus, overcoming the setback caused by Gandhi's murder by a Hindu extremist. The Gandhian ethos weakened over the years and the RSS found a leader who could polarise the nation on the religious lines. Hindus feel insecure, partly due to the constant warnings by the BJP politicians that they are in danger. The majority community has lost self-confidence. The minority community feels besieged. A ruthless and unfair regime has worsened the internal security situation. An instrument for tracking mental pollution would show a horrendous reading. The social media lies have increased general ignorance. Millions have passed out from the WhatsApp University, equipped with ignorance and lies.

The Text-book Fascist

Modi understands prejudices of fellow Indians and manipulates the masses. His qualities were known years before he became a chief minister and the Gujarat killings took place. Clinical psychologist Ashis Nandy, who interviewed Modi when he was an ordinary RSS *pracharak,* was shaken by what he heard from Modi. After the meeting, Nandy said he had seen a 'classic, clinical text-book case of a fascist and a prospective killer'. A decade after that interview, the killings of Muslims in Gujarat yielded political dividend for chief minister Narendra Modi. He got consecrated as *Hindu Hriday Samrat,* the Emperor of Hindu Hearts. It was because of this history that many Indians, including this writer, were filled with unease as the 2014 parliamentary elections approached. During the poll campaign, stray voters confirmed that Modi had indeed become the Emperor of Hindu Hearts. It increased one's misgivings. Something is not right when children in an auto-rickshaw say: *Modi aajaay to achha hoga, unko fix kar dega.* (It will be good if Modi is elected, he will fix them.) They repeat what they hear from their parents at home.

This reporter heard the same words from two voters. It was clear why many wanted Modi to be the Prime Minister. And Modi, with his rich experience in Gujarat, knew what he was wanted for. Within days, I get a disconcerting message in New Delhi's elite club. While having lunch in a group, I am asked about Modi. 'As Prime Minister, he would be a disaster', I say, expecting a logical rebuttal. No argument follows. The friend just asks me to go away to Pakistan. I share this incident with Gopal Gandhi who writes in *Hindustan Times*: 'In a venue known for its liberal and secular ambience, veteran columnist L K Sharma was bluntly told by a gentleman, "Go to Pakistan". 'LK' as he is known in his wide circle of friends, was, of course, in distinguished company. The celebrity actors Aamir Khan and Shah Rukh Khan have been similarly advised. And this same 'order' of exile to Pakistan was issued to the extraordinary thinker and writer U R Ananthamurthy. The 'order' was accompanied by hate mail, hate calls and physical intimidation.' In New India, contrarian thought is called anti-national, subversive, and treasonable. Intolerance of dissent or thought dons the garb of patriotism, says Gandhi.

Having transformed society in Gujarat through religious polarisation, Modi used the same formula at the national level. Before Gandhi's Gujarat was sullied by sectarian hatred, one had observed the gentle and helpful people there. In 1969, Gujarat saw deadly Hindu-Muslim violence. Then Gujarati Hindus felt apologetic and said: 'We did not do it. The jobless migrant textile mill workers of UP, *Bhaiyyas*, did the killings.' But in 2002, the Gujarati women went around in cars looting Muslim properties. During the 1969 communal violence in Ahmedabad, this reporter, sporting a beard, went home from the office every night on a scooter. This would have been dangerous in 2002.

Modi, in his 2014 election campaign, promised to protect Hinduism and its gods from imagined assaults by a minority. Hinduism that had continued to flourish under the long alien rule and in independent India was categorised as 'endangered'. Hindu voters in the parliamentary elections knew of Modi's performance as the chief minister during the communal killings of 2002 that established his religious credentials. Modi's demagoguery made the voters ignore his sins of omission and commission. Many became Modi's blind followers, consolidating his hold on political power.

Could India have a *Hindu Hridhay Samrat* as its Prime Minister? The people gave their answer in 2014. Misgivings of secular Hindus were not shared by the majority of voters. Modi won the 2014 elections and became the Prime Minister of a vastly diverse country, India. This writer told his friend, 'I don't have to go to Pakistan, you will turn India into Pakistan'. The temperature raised by the communal virus in 2002 developed into a raging high fever. The Curse of 2014 poisoned the body politic. Liberal Hindus were shocked. Eminent author Pankaj Mishra wrote that the result of the nastiest election campaign announced the 'most sinister' turbulent phase since independence from British rule in 1947. Back then, he wrote in *The Guardian,* it would have been inconceivable that a figure such as Narendra Modi, an accused of complicity in crimes, barred from entering the US, may occupy India's highest political office. Modi went on to do that not once but three times!

Modi Comes to Delhi

Serenaded by the corporate *band-baja*, Modi entered the Prime Minister's office in New Delhi. Modi's victory in parliamentary elections resulting from the consolidation of Hindu votes empowered his followers to punish 'The Other'. In many cases, the state colluded with them. Modi has used state power to intimidate opponents and media, making the Republic of Fear a functioning entity. Modi's boast of his chest size, advocacy of muscular Hinduism, suppression of dissent, curtailment of civil liberties, and surveillance of citizens, seem to herald a strong state. In reality, this state is guided by this collective psyche, a supposedly 'Hindu' worldview that dictates what the Government can do and not do. Modi has to ensure that no bigger 'Hindu' comes up in his party to challenge him. Ever fearful of hurting this 'Hindu psyche', Modi did not have the option of cancelling a Hindu religious fair despite the Corona epidemic. The state fears 'Hindus' "awakened" by the Modi Machine! The drumbeat of placating the Hindu psyche becomes a deafening roar during election campaigns!

As the Prime Minister, Modi influenced even some accredited liberals who wrote what was lapped up by the Modi fans. While Modi was waiting in the wings, some prominent ones had gone hammer-and-tongs after the Manmohan Singh Government, failing to anticipate what would come next, with their writing paving the path for the Modi juggernaut. Even the tiny section of the media that could not be bought or bamboozled did the balancing act, giving equal opportunities to lies and truthful statements! A secular columnist, taken up with Modi, was featured by a magazine as one of the four 'Modi's Maidens'. She, like some liberal academics, later realised what Modi was doing to India. She had seen an unreal Modi because she had not asked the simple question: Where does this leader come from? The answer had enabled this non-academic to see the coming Age of Hate.

Modi's image remains unsullied by the BJP's acquisition of real estate throughout the country and the hi-tech luxurious headquarters in New Delhi. His crony capitalism got worldwide publicity because he has been granting special favours to one big business tycoon. Even when a newspaper exposes a financial scam involving the Government or a dodgy contract or import deal, the Opposition is unable to engineer moral panic. It lacks the cadres to match the RSS network. Corruption has found liberalised India even more hospitable than the socialist India. Naturally, world leaders have to deal whoever is the Prime Minister of India. They said Modi meant business and business mattered to them. Growing majoritarianism did not matter. They did business with a whimsical leader who was not accountable. They showered praise on Modi, overlooking his disastrous moves. The US had cancelled Modi's visa because of the Gujarat killings but restored it gladly when he became the Prime Minister.

Age of Hate

The direction in which the Prime Minister has pushed India frightens a very large section of her population. It watches the mob-lynching of beef traders and beef eaters, a violent campaign against 'love jihad', trolling of dissenters and independent journalists, jailing of activists, comedians and scholars, attacks on women in bars and a systematic degradation of institutions including universities. The general degradation of public life has been caused by the nature of the person while his policies have led to tragic consequences. We always had base instincts such as hatred, fear, tribalism and outrage had always been there but then came a leader who industrialized these.

Modi's demonetisation caused misery to millions but he applauded its shock value, and in the Uttar Pradesh State election campaign, incited the poor against the rich, ignoring his ties with the latter! Modi won the U P State elections despite demonetisation. Bihari migrant workers suffered due to his nation-wide Covid lockdown and still the BJP managed to come to power in Bihar, in alliance with a leader who won the election by opposing the BJP. Modi's reputation is not affected by his disastrous decisions.

The BJP's claim that it will win every election and rule for the next 50 years is designed to spread the aura of invincibility that has taken Modi quite far. Millions believe Modi. If told what ails India, his social media warriors shoot back: What about the ills when so and so was the Prime Minister? They resort to whataboutry to respond to any attack on him. Every Government had wanted votes, but this Government wants more than votes. It wants to control your mind and your personal life. It seeks the possession of mind-space, says political strategist Prashant Kishor. Steve Biko, antiapartheid activist, once said: 'The most potent weapon in the hands of the oppressor is the mind of the oppressed.' A large number of Indians have mortgaged their minds to Modi. Kishor should know Modi well because at one stage, he had helped him.

Modi does face political setbacks, but a marginal defeat never bothers him because the BJP is able to attract defectors to put together a majority. Before the West Bengal elections, Modi managed to get some key members of the chief minister's Trinamool Congress defect to the BJP. Most of them were fielded as BJP candidates. Modi poured all his energy and corporate money into the West Bengal elections. The political din generated by the BJP turned the Covid tragedy into a non-issue. Modi pitted himself against chief minister Mamata Banerjee during the election campaign. He sneered at Mamata Didi. The Hindutva card was played more wildly as the BJP leaders kept calling Mamata Banerjee, Mamata Begum. Modi stooped to vulgarity by shouting, *Didi-ohh-Didi,* in a tone used by roadside Romeos to tease a girl. Mamata Banerjee fought off the mighty forces descending on her state and dashed the BJP's dream of coming to power in West Bengal. In 2021, the Bengali voters, Hindus, Muslims and all others, were not swayed by the Modi cult or by the slogan of *Jai Shri Ram.* They were angered by Modi's mockery of Mamata. Mamata assumed the office of the chief minister for the third term. The voters of West Bengal denied oxygen to Modi and gave it to the gasping democracy instead. The next State election is due in 2026.

This setback led Modi to further intensify polarisation and more assaults on the constitutional institutions. Social media got suffused with messages of communal hatred, warning Hindus that their religion and their nation are endangered. Assam, which the BJP won, is being described as a 'nationalist' State. A former Congress leader who defected to the BJP made that victory possible. The States that reject the BJP in elections are maligned. West Bengal is called Bangladesh and Tamil Nadu is called Sri Lanka, as they both rejected the BJP. The Modi devotees will, no doubt, soon find a name for the communist-ruled Kerala where a BJP leader said he was helpless because of the 'high literacy rate' in the State. As per his logic, India must be kept semi-literate, that is in darkness, if the BJP is to win elections.

The *Jai Shri Ram* slogan did not work in West Bengal but later saw Modi through in the vast Hindi belt. His call makes those suffering pain experience it as pleasure on the voting day! They go through any misery caused by him without a murmur, if asked to do it in the service of the nation! His kind of report card would have destroyed any leader. In a western democracy, barring America, the party would have thrown out a leader for making one communal statement of the kind which Modi makes. With his quasi-religious appeal, Modi continues to prosper. For this quality, some western leaders were called Teflon-coated as no dirt stuck to them.

With funeral fires raging in May 2021 because of the broken health infrastructure, the BJP-RSS activists put out 'positive' posts and conspiracy theories to suppress the growing disenchantment. With such misgovernance by the Leader, any party would have split. Not the BJP. Its workers are trained by the RSS not to question the Leader. Modi knew the funeral pyres seen around the world will not singe his political career. For one decade, Prime Minister Modi's decisions extracted heavy human costs but his 'Magic Man' cult lost no followers. Modi was not held accountable. Watch a leader who lights a fire and emerges from the flames laughing!

After 2014, Indians saw normalisation of intolerance, bigotry, hatred, and strife. Modi's cultural revolution undermined rational thinking. India's social fabric was torn asunder and democracy started faltering. Its ranking in the areas of freedom of speech and free press has fallen. Social development indices are pathetic. The term 'Hindu terror' diminished the reputation of Hinduism. The word 'fascism' began to feature in political discourse in 1992 when Prof. Ashis Nandy, noted clinical psychologist, interviewed Narendra Modi, then an ordinary RSS functionary, and diagnosed him to be a 'textbook fascist'. Within a few years, the party made him the chief minister! The Gujarat model of hate was popularised nationwide.

Nandy's prophetic words about Modi are today examined closely and the word 'fascism' is not bandied about casually. Many Indians see a civilised democracy turning into an authoritarian state. They recall the past Germany and ask: 'Can it not happen here?' A German character in Nayantara Sahgal's novel tells his Indian friend: *Our past is your future.* The Jews in Germany were undistinguishable from Christians, sartorially, socially, economically. Muslims in India are not. Moreover, data science was not advanced in the thirties. In Gujarat, in 2002, the arsonists, armed with voters lists and petrol, identified the houses for burning. Moving accounts of bestiality against the Muslim women in Ahmedabad appeared in journals. A Hindu writer saw 'sinister signs of an utterly cynical man planning his rise to power, using his pseudo Hinduism to fool the people'. Liberal Hindus lamented that they failed in the face of such brutality. Since it was done in the name of Hinduism, they wondered why they did not scream: 'This is not our faith'. A Hindu writer said, 'the shameful thing we discover about ourselves is that we are afraid. We cannot be sure we will not be betrayed by a watching eye and punished because we have aided the Muslims. It is now possible to understand what happened in Germany'. That was 2002. And no lessons were learnt.

Indians keep sinking in the sea of misinformation. Educated Indians deride Nehru for 'being a Muslim and Indira Gandhi for marrying a Muslim'. A young fact-checker investigates and puts the stamp of 'False' on photoshopped images and fabricated videos. He pays for his 'crime' as cases are filed against him. Many journalists are in jail or on bail! New India is not a fairyland but a FIRland. FIRs are filed against eminent citizens for 'insulting' the Prime Minister by writing to him. Their crime is worse than rape; it is like when a raped woman goes to a police station to file an FIR and, she is thrown out for harassing a reputed man. Every police station perhaps has boxes labelled 'Insulting Prime Minister' and 'Hurting Hindu Psyche' for storing these FIRs. The judiciary helps the filers of such FIRs. A court ordered that FIR be filed against 49 celebrities who 'insulted' the Prime Minister by writing a letter to him. In 2019, Ramachandra Guha, Shyam Benegal, Aparna Sen, Amit Chaudhuri, Mani Ratnam, Adoor Gopalakrishnan, Shubha Mudgal, Anurag Kashyap and others 'committed the crime'. The FIRs, under IPC sections, related to sedition, breach of peace and hurting religious sentiments, were lodged at the Muzaffarpur Sadar police station. These were filed on an order passed by a Chief Judicial Magistrate while hearing a petition by a social activist and lawyer who alleged that the accused persons had tarnished India's image and undermined the Prime Minister's impressive performance, and supported secessionist tendencies. Gopalakrishnan said the issues raised by them should have been examined but instead of that, a complaint was registered against them! He pointed out that the Government and the judiciary missed seeing people shooting an effigy of Mahatma Gandhi!

Because of such FIRs, many journalists have spent years attending court hearings in distant parts of India. Some public-spirited people, living in the past, want to improve things by writing letters to editors. A group of anguished retired top officials, eminent artistes and scholars regularly write to Prime Minister Modi, expressing concern over the atrocities against the poor and the steady erosion of Constitutional values. Gagaland's giant office bin devours such letters. The dutiful citizens are not discouraged and keep drafting and signing the next letter. The Opposition leaders say the Constitution is in danger and Modi's men shout: 'Hindus are in danger'. The former regret the erosion of constitutional morality but this remains an abstract issue for the people who love the Leader. Thus the principle-based poll campaign by the opposition yields no political benefits.

Infotainment is new journalism, with governments and social groups generating comic material. As a knowledge society, India has regressed but the Leader keeps claiming that India has become *Vishwa Guru*, the teacher of the universe. History is destroyed along with old monuments. Historians are trolled. The tirade against intellectuals and the state's action against academics invite international criticism. Foreign academics rally round the persecuted faculty members. The education system is in shambles, universities have been enfeebled. Leading universities such as the JNU, Jamia and Delhi University, Jadavpur and AMU have become the prime targets. Education correspondents used to cover universities but now crime correspondents are needed to report events there. Headlines of their reports in the independent media tells the story: '*They were banging the door with an iron rack': Students, teachers describe JNU violence. 'Bloody Sunday': A University in Grave Crisis.*

Chokehold: Law and disorder stifling dissent in Jamia Millia Islamia. Police Violence in Jamia and Aligarh Muslim University. Delhi University as a microcosm of a police state. Urgent need to save knowledge institutions from majoritarianism. What is ailing the South Asian University and how to save it. Like America's Republican Party, the BJP wants to demolish the cradles of dissent and reason. All rightwing populist leaders have similar traits and adopt a somewhat common political strategy. They inculcate blind faith among the masses to protect them from rationalism. The Hindutva leaders call Liberal Hindus 'sick' and send vigilantes after them. The murdered rationalists were Hindus.

In the Republic of Fear, an intimidated Gauri abandons her idol Khan instead of marrying him. Inter-faith love wilts due to threats on social media and at times, physical attacks and complaints to the police. Such couples intending to marry run away from their State and even then, are chased by the police and family members. A Hindu wife has to rent a house in her name, hiding from the landlord that her husband is Muslim. Muslim housemaids use Hindu names to get domestic work. Some young men discard their beard and skull caps that can invite an unprovoked attack. Studies will show that anxiety levels have risen, and the mental health of Indians has deteriorated.

Modi's giant experiment to modify the secular democratic India as well as tolerant Hinduism is seen but ignored by the western governments supposed to be committed to democracy! With stakes in India, their strategic partner, they focus on the 'economic opportunity' held out by India. The US believes India is doing well, though its media at times gives thumbs down to Modi.

Western scholars come to study India's great transformation. Sociologists, political scientists, anthropologists, and mass psychologists land in India in droves. After one scholar was denied the Indian Visa for research, they come as tourists. Here they study crony capitalism, tribalism, identity politics, populism, polarisation, repression, religious right-wing, oligarchy, mobocracy, kleptocracy, plutocracy, elected autocracy, rising aristocracy and dying democracy.

Western business leaders salivate seeing this large market for their goods and services. They ignore the freedom fora reports on India. Similarly, Indian business leaders see Trump doing no harm to Americans and hold seminars on big new business opportunities in Trump's America.

Modi's rise as the Supremo is mainly attributed to his religious polarisation project that consolidated Hindu votes. Those not driven by sectarian hatred rallied behind Modi by the false propaganda about his 'Gujarat Development Model'. An unusual nexus between capitalism and communalism was formed. The neoliberal policies of the previous Congress-led governments encouraged big business to influence government policies. Chief Minister Narendra Modi won over the big business by granting incentives. Massive transfers of public resources into private hands began in lieu of the business houses financing Modi's election campaigns. Some commentators say that Prime Minister Modi is a puppet in the hands of his giant businessman friends who really rule India.

Hollywood Hindus

Strangely, in this *Amrit Kaal* more Indians are migrating to foreign shores, to practice long-distance patriotism. The intellectual NRIs critical of Modi are called anti-national. No devout Modi devotee has asked his NRI son to return to the motherland. Prime Minister Modi commands a huge following among Hindus living outside India. Unsure of their identity, they are attracted to the Hindutva ideology. Some sent gold bricks for the Ram Mandir in Ayodhya. Their enthusiasm was reflected in the massive rallies that Modi addressed in the UK and USA. Modi's poll campaign for Trump in Houston in 2020 (*abki baar Trump Sarkar)*, projecting his giant-sized image, electrified the Indian diaspora. India's diplomatic missions deploy the diaspora for Modi's visits. The NRI crowds are assembled at the airport to cheer Modi when he alights.

V S Naipaul, who observed Hindus in America, called them 'Hollywood Hindus'. They are known as

'Keyboard Patriots' and 'FB Nationalists'. Ironically, the NRIs want an extra liberal regime in the country of their adoption but want India suffused with hatred and bigotry that characterise Hindutva. They want Modi to rule India but not America. Now that they have got a Modi-like POTUS, Am-Indians are worried about their future there. Trump's polarisation project and damning of the illegal immigrants perturb the Indian diaspora. Pregnant Indian women flocked to hospitals for pre-term caesarean section deliveries, so that the baby does not miss the deadline after which babies born to non-citizens in the USA would be denied citizenship.

Modi has been lucky. The new international political climate helped him in a big way. 9/11 caused a disaster in the US but brought luck to Modi. The powerful West looked for and co-opted an Islamophobic ally in the South. The US approves of Modi's approach towards Muslim citizens because it needs Islamophobic countries as partners. Before 9/11, a single Kashmiri Muslim's death at the hands of the security forces used to enrage American and British legislators. Such deaths became a non-issue by the time Modi assumed office in Delhi.

9/11 destroyed the West's concern for civil liberties in India. America believes that a supernatural Indian can help it fight China and Russia. As the far Right made headway in the US and Europe, odd White influencers cropped up, denouncing Islam, supporting Hindutva in India and popularising elements of Hinduism such as

Yoga and Ayurveda in their Christian countries. With the upsurge of the religious right-wing there, Modi came into political fashion. He is not alone; he basks in the comfortable company of his soulmate in a Christian country. God's messengers lead the largest democracy and the oldest democracy. One ushers in the *Amrit Kaal*, the other ushers in the Golden Age. In the US, the Republican Party gave up its principles to support Trump. In India, the RSS gave up its principles to support its pupil in power. Trump and Modi can be seen as soul siblings. One says he would make America great again. The other says the same about India. Every exploration of the Polarised India leads to the Nonbiological Being who transformed his own self and is committed to transform a country and even an ancient faith known as Hinduism.

Ordinary to Extraordinary

When he became the Prime Minister, a Mumbai newspaper called Narendra Modi, 'God of all he surveys'. It was right because like Lord Shiva, Modi assimilates in his person all contradictions. His election campaign speeches contain contradictions galore. It is impossible to know what Modi believes in. Some Indians want the real Modi to stand up but he never obliges them. He has the quality that any politician would kill for. 'The ability to make substance irrelevant' is what an American politician called it. So, issues that matter are rendered irrelevant and non-issues take up all the time of the media and politicians in India.

The story of these years in India is of an ordinary man who acquired extraordinary powers, using his wits to win the hearts of Indians. Modi came to Delhi and got going to implement the majoritarian agenda, changing his sartorial make-up, roaming the global stage, hugging the high and mighty to impress Indians back home. He demolished opponents with mockery and sneering. He awakened the baser instincts of the masses and empowered fanatic groups. Modi centralised hold on power, enfeebling his Cabinet and mentors in the BJP. The Prime Minister takes decisions that cause human suffering but he does not have to pay any political price. This further boosts his self-confidence. The versatile leader, bathed in public adoration, brought to office a rare package of talents. He keeps the data ready for his Polarisation Project. Narendra Modi plays a variety of roles. He knows choreography, theatrical entrances and exits, sartorial devices, masks, camera angles, and quick responses. His mentor called him the 'best events manager'!

Modi perfected the piety-profits-politics business model with the Ram Mandir as its key element. For those unimpressed by his Godman-like qualities, he has a different message: 'I am a Gujarati. Business is my business.' The business leaders rally behind him. He demonetised currency notes and monetised faith. He endears himself to the temple owners by sending more devotees and to tycoons through land grants and permission grants. As to the media moguls and so-called journalists, what will they not do for a Rajya Sabha nomination! Modi proves that there is no one who cannot be bought or bullied. Modi displays his spiritual leaning to attract the believers. He organised his meditation to be photographed and circulated. He projected himself as a quasi-religious leader and got politically rewarded for it. Knowing the political clout of Godmen, Modi promised to conjure up good times from thin air. He and his followers see to it that in public imagination, his visage and that of the Divine merge like a GIF image. The BJP gave Modi the divine status and he anointed himself as a Nonbiological Being with a 56-inch chest! Perhaps he took the cue from one of his followers who built a temple with Modi's idol! The faithful suffer the Government-made disasters as divine retribution but see accidental benefits as boons granted by Modi. The Covid vaccine certificate carried Modi's photo! Only one person refused to take the vaccine unless his photo was removed from the certificate!

Modi yoked together two antithetical forces – capitalism and communalism. BJP's communalism should have hampered Modi in wooing the capitalists but Indian capitalists are generally short-sighted as they focus on short-term gains. They ignore the dangers of communalism and help in its propagation even though most of them are not sectarian. To many, Modi presented himself as a valiant son of Mother

India. To the chosen few who mattered, he portrayed himself as a creature of the Corporate India. The two faces fitted into his electoral strategy as he promised majoritarianism and crony capitalism. The voters were convinced that he would strengthen their Hindu identity by showing the other community its place. India Inc. was convinced that his pro-business and anti-environment policies would raise their stocks sky-high. It opened purse strings and underwrote his mega poll campaigns. It created the myth of the 'Gujarat model of development' that white-washed Modi's failures as the chief minister of the State that witnessed a communal massacre.

Modi is obsessed with political power and his brand image. He projects himself as a strong man who shocks the system at will. He excels in public performance. Marlon Brando said politicians are actors of the first order. Modi is the top star. The tragedy of India cannot be understood without observing Modi's personal traits. His personality shapes his governance style. Governance suffers because of Modi's disregard for expert opinion. He makes it clear that he knows all and he takes all decisions, running a presidential form of government that has made his elected cabinets redundant. Most ministers have been assigned only one task, which is to keep tweeting in praise of the Prime Minister in the midst of a humanitarian disaster. An insider's view of Modi as an administrator is given by a noted civil servant who resigned as he could not cope with the transformation that the Prime Minister initiated. Jawhar Sircar witnessed 'the collapse of the apparatus of governance, which invariably invites catastrophe of the type we are suffering now'. He writes in *The New Indian Express*: Modi's micro-management caused a problem and officials hoped in vain that having reached the pinnacle, Modi would deactivate his suspicious nature and curb his urge to centralise powers and demand unquestioned obedience. Narendra Modi revealed his 'control-freak' nature and deliberately kept bypassing his ministers and started operating through his favourites. Sircar says lightning transfers became commonplace in the early years and Modi's office controlled every appointment. Inputs were taken from the RSS, Intelligence Bureau, and the spy chief. 'Stalinist shadows grew longer. Babus and businessmen, however, learnt to fake everlasting loyalty and started wooing the RSS men. The Cabinet system crashed and responsibility became opaque. Regular imperious edicts followed.'

Having an elephantine ego, Modi built a massive Government building complex including a palatial Prime Minister's residence served by an underground transit system. While all non-essential projects were stopped as per the Covid protocol, this construction was declared an 'essential service'. The British *Daily Mail* called it a monstrous monument to Narendra Modi's ego – a vast folly being built at a cost that could fund 40 major hospitals. Modi is obsessed with his image.

Modi gets away with lies. He distorts language, changes meanings, and turns respectable words into terms of abuse. Modi rewards loyalists. He uses and discards mentors and is lauded for that by selfish society. He outwitted a cultured Prime Minister of his own party, who wanted him to resign as the chief minister of Gujarat in the wake of communal violence there. Modi has gone on to believe even more in the power of his dramatic gestures and shock decisions. Modi bewitches the people with rhetoric, mockery of his opponents and insulting allusions to a minority. His sign language protects him from prosecution for spreading communal hatred. He sneers and entertains with dramatic gestures. The Twitter-Age politician instils the fear of 'The Other'. Modi makes people respond to his questions and calls. When he asks them, they come out banging utensils and lighting candles. When he asks them, they faint in long queues to get cash from the banks. When he asks them, they walk for miles without food and water. His words touch the heartstrings and make the people feel that they are suffering for a worthy case. Everyone is out to be classified as a patriot and avoid the stigma of being called anti-national. Modi is an illusionist who has turned Indians into delusionists! The great orator knows how they would respond if he were to ask them in his pet style: 'Doesn't the sun rise in the west? Doesn't the sun rise in the west?' 'It does. It does', roars the mesmerised crowd! The keyboard patriots and FB nationalists repeat the same.

Modi presents his handicaps as virtues, and what he lacks and his opponents have, is projected as despicable traits and flawed legacies. So, higher education, intellectual prowess, pedigree, political work and public service by one's forefathers, cultural inheritance and decent upbringing are 'undesirable' features of India's political life that he cleans up. Modi claims to fight the 'elite' but has established a nexus of big business and the new political elite. The close state-capital alliance is Modi's achievement. The rampant crony capitalism is noticed only by the alternative media. The judiciary and administration have been subverted through offers of plum assignments to retired judges and civil servants. In an election rally, Modi talked of *kabristan* (Muslim graveyard) and *shamshan* (Hindu crematorium) to charge the Opposition with appeasement of Muslims. He said the gathering of miscreants can be recognised by the clothes of the participants (a dig at a Muslim crowd). The inhuman response to the farmers' agitation and mishandling of the pandemic exposed Modi as an incompetent leader, indifferent to human suffering and obsessed with expanding his fiefdom. But whenever Modi begins to gasp after his failure, some development pumps oxygen into his lungs.

A Faustian Bargain

The Modi years will be known for the modification of Hinduism and of the idea of India. Modi redefined democracy and turned India into a majoritarian state.

Seduced by a Faustian bargain, the people let him play with India's constitution and civil liberties. Modi just ignores an Opposition leader saying that he has blood on his hands and a newspaper calling him a 'shameless demagogue' and 'vainglorious man'. Modi is described as a narcissistic cult leader. A big cricket stadium is named after Narendra Modi, reminding his critics of Hitler. Having achieved all that he wanted in this life; Modi is trying to ensure that the posterity remembers him in a way that he wants. His 'achievements' will be remembered for long. Modi created polarisation and social destabilisation. He framed his political contest as a grand conflict between patriots and anti-nationals. His warriors keep pumping in misinformation to harm his opponents. Modi's toolkit to influence public perception contains hate, envy, fear, and hope. The diversionary tactics have been used with success. Books recorded Modi's bizarre claims, his ever-changing dandyish appearance, his chest size and the strange tales of his childhood and early life. Modi is par excellence as a practitioner of photo-op governance and photo-op diplomacy. A book on child Narendra applauds his bravery in catching a live crocodile from the river! The grown-up Narendra is applauded for his inaction during Gujarat's communal killings in 2002. Then comes the year 2014, and he begins to rule the nation with a firm hand, establishing a majoritarian state. He widens India's social fault-lines through wink-wink communal campaigns. He bends officials and institutions to his will, doling out incentives and inculcating fear. Without taking recourse to any official order, he diminishes democracy and curtails civil liberties. It is called an 'undeclared Emergency'.

Modi rejigged politics with a toolkit not acquired in any university. Without having read Nietzsche, Modi made *ressentiment* the centrepoint of his politics. It is a reassignment of the pain that accompanies one's own inferiority and failure on to an external scapegoat. We feel so worthless that we look for someone to blame and someone to save us. The Leader promises to protect us from the Other, our 'enemy'. Seduced, we bay for the blood of the scapegoat and vote for Modi. Modi understands India's social and religious fault-lines; he took the Ram Mandir campaign to its climax and kept us engrossed with the Mandir-Masjid drama. Eminent Hindi writer Prem Chand had written a story on mandir and masjid to highlight inter-faith harmony in a village. The current Mandir-Masjid serial is designed to create sectarian hostility. Its viewership leaps up during the election season, with abundant supply of horror and absurdity.

Our Spectacle Society created a creature who became its master. We lost belief in 'We' and reposed our trust in 'I'. The 'I' ushered in a *de facto* Hindu State in which Hindu Supremacist mobs run 'love jihad' or lynch Muslims for storing beef. The state joins in, sending bulldozers to demolish Muslim houses. The fault lies in ourselves! Beguiled by the false promise of power and prosperity, and moved by sectarian hatred, we trample upon our own interests to keep him going.

The Hindutva activists, in league with the Government, divided every institution. Some Hindu religious leaders have been co-opted to repeat the *sarkari* views. Scholars are called Hinduphobic while *sarkari* scholars are raised through patronage. Even British imperialists could not devise such a perfect Divide-and-Rule plan. Bollywood, a messenger of inter-faith harmony, has been divided through an ugly campaign and by financing the *sarkari* filmmakers. By giving land grants to the corporates, the Prime Minister convinced them that he would fix the economy. But he got busy 'fixing' culture by unleashing a war. A polarised India was ushered in by Modi through innuendos, dog-whistle politics, and sign language inspiring hate for The Other. *Time* magazine in 2019 called Narendra Modi India's Divider-in-Chief.

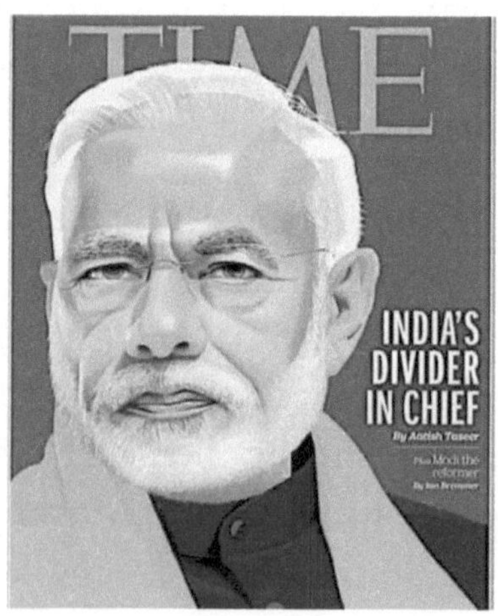

And in 2025, *Time* excluded Narendra Modi from the list of the 100 most influential persons of the world! He must have felt insulted.

In the Post-Truth India, the Leader's lies, dog-whistles, 'scientific' statements, distorting of names, giving new meanings to words and repeating funny equations impress the people. The Leader amuses them with vulgar speeches, wordplay, and sneering. They had applauded him when during the previous Government, he said the Rupee was in the ICU! That was before he came to Delhi. When as the Prime Minister, he moved the Rupee from ICU to the deathbed, the TV anchors ignored the poor Rupee.

Performance politics matters because Indian voters want to be entertained, not informed. How do journalists interpret the Leader's use of condescending sneer as a weapon of choice against the Opposition leaders? The Leader addresses a woman chief minister as *Didi-O'-Didi* and the non-Bengali reporters do not know that it is how a road Romeo teases a girl on the street. The Leader distorts language and names of his opponents. He calls one *Pappu* and Shahzada. He had blamed Prime Minister Manmohan Singh for his alleged silence and called him *Mounmohan* Singh. He had 'praised' Singh for knowing the 'art of bathing in the bathroom, wearing a raincoat'!

Doomsday Prophecies

Modi's rise generated plenty of literature warning the nation. One learns from literature. But what can one learn in a constantly frenzied state? Not all were taken in by Modi's deceptive words. Journalist Kapil Komireddi took a dim view of Modi's leadership. When Modi made a second bid in 2019, he warned that five more years of Narendra Modi will take India to a dark place. He wrote in *The Guardian* that Modi's sectarian politics will make bigotry the defining ideal of the republic. He reported the identical refrain from Hindu voters: 'Yes, Modi has failed us but he has at least put Muslims in their place.'

Some 15 books on Modi's India have been classified by activist Harsh Mander as 'books of conscience, books of courage, books of pain'. Komireddi's *Malevolent Republic* says the India founded in 1947 is dead. Rahul Bhatia's *The Identity Project: The Unmaking of a Democracy* traces the growth of Hindu nationalism, culminating into the breaking of the sacred compact between citizens and the state and a situation in which the government is attempting to choose its electorate.

The Republic Relearnt by Radha Kumar presents the defining features of Modi Raj: One nation, as defined by the RSS, dismantling of federalism, governance by a single leader using shock-and-awe tactics, destruction of independent media and grooming of 'fan media', disenfranchising of minorities and building a police state by weaponising the legislation against terrorism and using the police against opponents and critics.

Dhirendra K Jha in *Shadow Armies* says, 'the BJP's steady advance from two Lok Sabha seats in 1984 to 282 in 2014 has been accompanied by organisations that polarise, incite violence and even kill – all in the name of Hindutva'. Jha investigates and profiles eight fringe organisations across India that provide foot soldiers to the BJP.

The Crooked Timber of New India is a collection of essays written between 2020 to 2022 by economist Parakala Prabhakar. He gives extensive data on the downward trends of India's economy as well as social indices resulting from the Modi Government's acts of commission and omission. More worrisome, even frightening, is his analysis of the social deformation that will be Modi's toxic legacy. Prabhakar says: "This government willfully squanders our demographic dividend by filling the minds of young Indians with violent prejudice. Millions of our young citizens now confuse patriotism with blind past-worship, militarism, aggressive religious identity and uncritical support for the ruling party and its shrill, bombastic leaders. They become the foot soldiers of violent Hindutva without the capacity for independent thought and, tragically, without self-respect, having merged their personalities with the state and the Supreme Leader. They cannot build anything; they can only demolish and destroy." He says a majoritarian regime militates against social cohesion and thus disables a nation, rendering it incapable of delivering economic development to the people. The crooked timber of New India disallows the fostering of harmony, celebration of diversity, strengthening of national integration – all of which are pre-requisites for a progressive and prosperous nation.

Essays in *Majoritarian State: How Hindu Nationalism is Changing India* investigate the main causes and consequences of the illiberal turn taken by the world's largest democracy. The scholars explore how Hindutva ideology has permeated the state apparatus and formal institutions, and how Hindutva activists exert control over civil society via vigilante groups, cultural policing, and violence. The book explains how groups and regions portrayed as 'enemies' of the Indian state are the losers in a new order promoting the interests of the urban middle class and business elites. "As this majoritarian ideology pervades the media and public discourse, it also affects the judiciary, universities, and cultural institutions, captured by Hindu nationalists. Dissent is silenced and debate increasingly sidelined as the press is muzzled or intimidated in the courts."

The book *I am on the Hit List: A Journalist's Murder and the Rise of Autocracy in India* by American author Rollo Romig is 'a gripping investigation into the mysterious assassination of journalist Gauri Lankesh, revealing the courage and vulnerability of those fighting the decline of democracy around the world'. A reviewer says: 'Romig uncovers a world of political extremists, fearless writers, organised crime, and shadowy religious groups. The epic narrative moves between a historic booksellers' district and brand-new high rises funded by IT wealth, to a secretive ashram in Goa and the kitchens of an international vegetarian restaurant chain.' A novelist could not have invented a plot more thrilling than this life story of a woman journalist!

Several book titles characterise this New India. *Price of the Modi Years, Modi's India, The Malevolent Republic, India's Undeclared Emergency, The Incarcerations: Bhima Koregaon and the Search for Democracy in India, India's Soul Possessed, Ayodhya: The Dark Night, Shadow Armies, New India: The Unmaking of the World's Largest Democracy, Twilight Prisoners: The Rise of Hindu Right and the Decline of India, Democracy on Trial* and *Nothing Will be Forgotten.* All such books take us to one man who promised to eradicate hunger but fed the passions of citizens. He promised *achhe din* 'Good Days' that never came. The Gujarat Model of Development remained elusive while the Gujarat Model of Hate spread nation-wide, says economist Pranab Bardhan. Modi's pretensions of Godhood endangers what is left of India's democratic soul, says a commentator. The story of these toxic years is told in these books of conscience, investigative reports, and painful poems. It is told by shocking photos, viral tweets, amusing cartoons, and hate-filled Hindutva pop songs.

Much has been said about Modi's India. Some say the less said the better. Future historians will have diverse material about the Modi years because despite the curtailed freedom of speech, not all lips could be sealed. Denied space on the mainstream TV channels, many journalists took to social media to report the ground reality and express dissenting views. New technologies have enabled the subaltern to speak and to convey messages from villages to cities. Several writers, poets, and artistes defy a vengeful regime, heeding Hindi poet Ramdhari Singh Dinkar's warning that time will record the crimes of those who remain neutral (between Good and Evil). Dinkar's call makes them speak out.

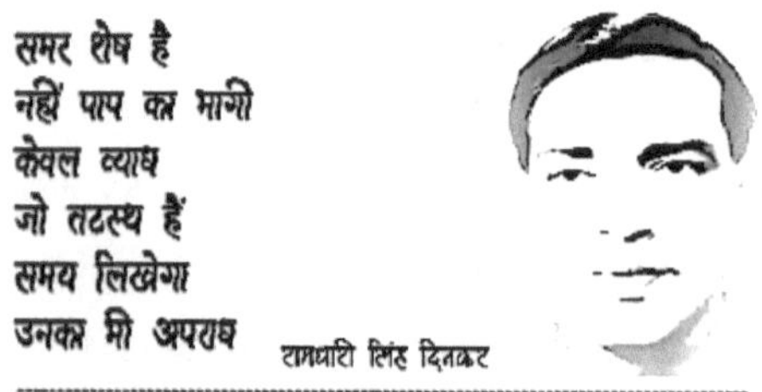

For several years, the tragedies caused by Modi's decisions and indifference did not make the populist leader less popular. Commentator Parakala Prabhakar explains: "The Prime Minister's political capital and communication skills seem to indemnify him from the impact of the incompetence and inaptitude of his Government. He is able to escape accountability. The Government and the ruling party are adept at outrage management. They understand that the initial sharp yelp after the pain will quickly be followed by the country becoming numb to suffering. They contained the fall-out of demonetisation because of this numbing. They could ride out the anger generated by the visuals of helpless migrant workers walking long distances, again because of this numbing. They are hoping to tide over the present mess-up also, expecting numbing yet again. But popularity and political capital have a habit of running out without notice. Communication skills, soon or late, begin to look like pantomimes and numbing will not last forever."

By 2024, more and more people began to admit that they got fooled by Modi. The economic decline and Covid mismanagement made them regret their political choice. Modi's style was ridiculed and lack of substance criticised. Posts condemned polarisation and Modi's gimmicks and lies. Social media carries satirical posts such as: 'If our family members are dying due to lack of medical facilities, why blame doctors. We did not vote for them. We did not demand hospitals. We wanted a temple to be built!' Several posts say that the people deserve the leader they get. A versifier points out that 'since we, the voters, gave credit to someone for communal killings, why mourn if funeral pyres burn all around us!' Another post: 'Who burnt our houses is not the question. We should be asking who gave the matchstick to a mad man.' Sampat Saral and other satirists say against Modi what the mainstream media do not say but the people want to hear. Stand-up comedians and poets got popular.

Modi must be thanked for the surge of creativity reflected in satirical poems and songs of resistance. With most of the audio-visual and print media turning into Modi's PR machine, individuals took to alternative media and social media for expressing revolutionary thoughts. The Modi Spectacle is becoming less attractive. His lies have begun to matter. The craftiest leader cannot fool all the people all the time. Even empires collapse. Modi did fail to win an absolute majority in the 2024 elections. The election results were widely hailed as a limited victory against dictatorship. Modi managed to become the Prime Minister for the third term by getting the support from two small parties. Modi's quasi-religious appeal will diminish further. His dramatic decisions and gestures, sartorial gimmicks, mendacity, threats and offers of sops – all will be rendered ineffective. Of course, it is difficult to say when the day of reckoning will come. Modi can subdue the craving for change by unleashing another 'surgical strike' against Pakistan, as per a tried and tested formula

The Godi media's power and influence have started diminishing. Modi's monopoly over social media has gone. Modi's critics in thousands have taken to social media. Those who live by social media, die by social media. Modi's past utterances haunt him. Posts condemn his crocodile tears, false promises, heartlessness, and relentless pursuit of political power in the midst of footpath funerals resulting from the collapsed health system.

The Toxic Legacy

The Leader empowered us to freely express hatred. Technology and Social media gave us anonymity to broadcast ugly thoughts without risk. Our naked brains grunt with spasms of communal prejudices, irrational thoughts, and desire to humiliate and harm the Other. He beckoned us and we discovered our depraved selves. He appeared like the iPhone, showing us what we want, awakening our mimetic desire steeped in religion and violence. His devotees and paid workers got us hooked on slanderous, inflammatory, and false online propaganda against his political opponents, purveyed by the WhatsApp University, to keep us occupied. The masses are distracted by non-issues in order to divert their attention from their problems. India is getting suffocated with poisonous gases pumped into the social system by sectarian politicians and blind followers. But moral decay does not affect the stock market and thus does not matter to those who matter. And in the past one decade, India has been taken over completely by those who matter while the commoners in large numbers have been turned into Hindutva warriors. Therein lies a big danger for a nation that has turned against itself.

The Emperor without clothes will be more ruthless. An empire in decline becomes crueller and more ludicrous. A leader out to memorialise himself with stadia, statues and grand buildings would do everything in his last days to prove: 'After me, the deluge'. Modi's army of political activists, trained to disturb social harmony, will not tolerate the rejection of their hero by the people. After all, they were told that BJP would win every coming election for the next 50 years. So, they would go berserk. A*chhe din* (good times) may not come even after Modi is gone. Some relief will come because hoodlums will no longer be empowered by the state. However, the BJP which in the Opposition had scuttled the functioning of Parliament, will play the disruptive game again. India will have to cope with Modi's toxic legacy. No decent politician stands a chance now because the people have lost appetite for reasoned conversations and nuanced statements. They have got addicted to political porn and perpetual confrontation. They would want more drama and more cockfights in the TV talk shows. They would want public threats against Pakistan.

Lies and rumours have become defining features of Indian life. The era of misinformation will not end because, as an expert says, an 'ingrouping' has taken place. The people have come to believe that their religious identity is a source of their strength and superiority, and that other groups are to be blamed for their problems. Brendan Nyhan, a noted political scientist, says the biggest culprit is social polarisation. 'At the mass level, greater partisan divisions in social identity are generating intense hostility toward Opposition partisans', which has increased the political system's vulnerability to partisan misinformation. The regime will change but no new official document will erase the belief that Nehru was a Muslim and Indira was married to a Muslim! The people have learnt these 'facts' from a million WhatsApp messages, videos and directly from respectable leaders. Many children now know that India gained freedom in 2014 and they will argue vehemently with those who make the mistake of saying 1947. Political pornography has corrupted India's soul. Standardised thinking and uniformity are in fashion now. Humans are afflicted with the zombie virus. The infantilisation of India cannot be reversed. Enfeebled, and compromised institutions will face a crisis that Modi's ideologically driven devotees will cause. A democratic successor will have to deal with mob violence by trained cadres. The steel frame (civil services) that protected India during the traumatic post-partition months, has collapsed. A de-Modifcaion drive will be beyond a new democratic leader.

Will the system, rigged for the benefit of the billionaires, be corrected? Modi facilitated the hijacking of democracy by corporate interests. Will they let their hold loosen easily or recruit the next Prime Minister? If a Prime Minister refuses to be dictated to, he is smeared, silenced and 'democratically' removed.

Will future elections be not decided by money? Some citizens have lost confidence in democracy. A few protest songs against Modi attack democracy itself. The Indian Army gets referred to as Modi's Army, as the Modi Government has made attempts to make the

Army march to the Hindutva tune. A few symptoms show that it is no longer inoculated against that virus. In some countries, military dictators ousted politicians. Hyper-extremism tends to follow extremism.

Will the clown show end and the image-world featuring the giant Leader be shattered? Will sanity and social harmony be restored in this polarised India? Will the poison be sucked out by a Gandhi-like cultural revolutionary?

As to the long-term consequences, according to Prof. Nandy, one generation of Indians will have to bear the cost of what Modi has done. The present drives many Indians to despair and they do not see a bright future either. Those who retain some hope point out that the targeted minority, due to its numerical strength, cannot be shoved into the ocean. This reality will force Indians to relearn to live together peacefully. India has civilisational resilience and true Hinduism will resurge to guide the people again. Time will tell.

MEANWHILE

MIND THE LEADER

Modi turns back the Wheel of Time

Consecrated in Ayodhya as *Dev-Raja* (God-King), Narendra Modi returned to his office in New Delhi to clear the files piled up due to his temple-hopping. Some humans accorded him the Divine status. An official of the Ramjanmabhoomi Trust declared that Modi is Lord Vishnu's avatar. Modi's idol was installed in the first *Modi Mandir* some years ago. If there is a Parliament of Hindu Gods, they may formally welcome a new entrant into their fraternity!

Scholars say the concept of God-King is rooted in the indigenous tradition. They used to say this about democracy! As someone says: "History is a fluid creature and easily contaminated.... authoritarian regimes edit and airbrush history books as the key to political legitimacy.... increasingly used to polarise society...." The narratives about the Babri Mosque and the Ramjanmabhoomi Movement validate this view.

The Prime Minister has emerged as an object of veneration. L K Advani, BJP's top leader, said Modi was chosen by God as his instrument for the Ayodhya event. "God's instrument" is a term used by Modi for himself in his election speeches. Time and again, he highlights his connection with the Divine. He hears the call of the Divine. One widely circulated poster shows the life-sized Modi escorting child Ram back to the temple.

The Union Cabinet members joined in the worship of the *Mahamanav* who presides over their meetings. They expressed their feeling of spiritual bliss "*aatmic anand*" flowing from Modi's feat. They adopted a resolution calling Modi the Harbinger of a New Era who achieved what the Indian civilisation had dreamt of for 500 years! The Cabinet Resolution, a devout Hindu said, has caught the spirit of a Sanskrit prayer to Lord Ganesh! He realised he had been praying to a wrong God1 The reverential Cabinet Resolution indicates that a New God has replaced an old one! One Modi critic is re-reading the biography of the North Korean "Dear Leader". Modi should not be blamed if he feels the pangs of grandeur.

Some called Modi the "fifth Shankaracharya" because he took the prime position at the religious ceremony. This goes against a basic tenet of Hinduism that each person should follow his or own *dharma*, specific duty, and conduct. The Raja should follow his *raj dharma* and a priest or saint should do his religious duties. But in this strange scenario, religious leaders are making political statements and a Prime Minister is lecturing on religious matters and talking of the Divine.

Modi mobilised the people all over India by calling upon them to light *diyas* on January 22. The BJP wants the "return" of Ram to be remembered by the masses till the coming parliamentary elections. Modi thinks big. He says the day will be remembered for a thousand years. He may announce that a time-capsule of the January 22 event will be buried deep in the ocean and planted on the moon! It may inform the future historian that a new *Treta Yug* began in 2014. In his speech at the consecration, Modi talked of *Kalachakra*. He did not explain whether it was simply a reference to the Wheel of Time or to the intricate Buddhist tantric practice. Modi's speech writer must have studied the generation stage of this practice involving the visualisation of oneself as a deity within the context of a *mandala*.

The Ayodhya spectacle was organised on a grand scale. The State played a big role. It deployed thousands of folk artistes to entertain the guests. Half a day's holiday was declared by government offices on January 22. Devotional songs were played on the TV channels and through loudspeakers. Life-sized cut-outs of Modi were seen hanging on the roadside poles. Millions of saffron flags were waved with exultation and with hostility towards "the other". The Prime Minister's wise words at the consecration were lost on the newly minted Ram devotees. Knowing what Modi stands for, they demonstrated fake religiosity on roads and in colonies without fearing police action. The local BJP leaders assured them of police inaction. A wave of triumphalism led them to shout provocative slogans in front of Muslims in Mumbai which led to violent clashes. Some mosques attracted mobs shouting that every child must say *Jai Shri Ram.* A wag asked the Government to build more mosques because what the Ram devotees like most is to chant outside mosques! Elsewhere, a Ram devotee climbed atop a church and planted a saffron flag above the Cross. A set pattern of organised lumpenisation and religious polarisation marks Indian democracy. Mobocracy is no longer a dirty word.

The Ayodhya spectacle served the purpose of energising Modi's electoral base through a religious show. Drowning in the rising sea of faith, Hindus admired the razzmatazz of the epoch-making politico-religious carnival. They were struck by Modi's sartorial elegance, his event management, and his effort to remain in front of the camera lens. Even while praying, he faces the camera while the idol is on his side. Modi hates to show his back to the camera. The shiny Ayodhya temple saw politicians, singers, dancers, decorators, celebrities, film stars, choreographers, speechwriters, saints, and billionaires. Masons and carpenters will be back to complete the temple. Some saints say that their work will defile the consecrated temple. Ayodhya's transformation has impressed all, barring those whose houses were destroyed for widening the roads. The demolition of small temples and mosques for the same purpose did not hurt religious sentiments this time! The temple town now has an airport and new luxury hotels. The Vatican will have to spruce itself, to compete with the Hindu Vatican.

After political Hindutva was unleashed 10 years ago, a wide gulf developed between liberal and conservative Hindus. The consecration divided even the devout Hindus. Modi's status in the ceremony was questioned by religious scholars who explained how consecration must be performed as per the sacred texts. Also, they questioned the decision to have it done in a temple that was incomplete. To telecast the image of the Prime Minister, the camera was allowed inside the sanctum-sanctorum of the new Ram Temple which shocked the traditionalists. Consolidation of the Hindu votes is an essential element of the BJP's electoral strategy. But the rituals at the Ram Temple caused a rift among the Hindus instead of uniting them. This division may do no harm to Modi as these traditionalists will not vote for a secular party.

Modi has reasons to be immensely satisfied with what he achieved by having the half-built temple consecrated before the parliamentary elections. Modi tracks his internal enemies and saw the challenge coming from Yogi Adityanath, fast emerging as a rival Hindutva icon. By demonstrating his pre-eminence in the temple, Modi cut the Yogi to size and ensured that the UP chief minster does not rob the *Hindu Hriday Samrat* crown from him. Even the RSS chief Mohan Bhagwat found it necessary to praise Modi for his *tapasya* preceding the ceremony. Bhagwat will stop looking for an alternative to Modi.

The roar of faith has sealed the people's ears to the voices of reason. Not to shout *Jai Shri Ram* is an anti-national act. Posters on social media warned those not going to Ayodhya on November 22: "You will commit a sin." An Age of Superstitions dawned. No Arya Samaj leader such as Swami Agnivesh countered such warnings. In the present atmosphere, no one will dare to write on how Ram behaved with his wife, a popular theme of feminist prose and poetry written in Hindi.

In this weird India, bizarre scenes are witnessed daily. Some feel embarrassed by all that is going on, such as an airline parading its crew dressed as Ram, Laxman and Sita or the Government buses playing songs in praise of Lord Ram! Those Hindus who are not attracted to Hindutva feel anguished about the mixing of religion with politics, violent assertion of majoritarianism, oppression of a minority and progressive destruction of India's secular Constitution. Many live in fear.

The governments focus on religious issues, doing little about poverty, hunger, and ill-health. A government hospital in Delhi decides to close for half a day because of the ceremony in the distant town of Ayodhya. It later withdraws that order in the face of protests. Many deprivileged Hindus keep telling the TV interviewers that they want jobs, hospitals, and schools, not temples. An old cartoon by R. K. Laxman shows the board of a Government-run "Temple and Mosque Construction Company", with the common man outside asking when the nation will be built!

The quest for personal power in India bordering on imperialism, makes one recall Rudyard Kipling's story and the famous film *The Man Who Would Be King*. The growing superstitions and tribalism and the emergence of a new God in India reminds him of Kafiristan. Kipling wrote about two British rogue soldiers who took over Kafiristan whose tribe, mesmerised by the white skin, anointed one of them as God. The white Britisher is subsequently found out because he marries a tribal woman. Out of fright, she bites him and his bleeding face makes the tribe realise that he is no God but a mortal.

Modi has ensured that the Indian diaspora does not remain untouched by his magic. Th wave of triumphalism reached distant lands and some Am-Indians in New York took out a procession hailing Ram and shouting an old slogan: "*Ayodhya to jhanki hai, Kashi, Mathura baaki hai*", reminding Indians that they must do the same to the mosques in Kashi and Mathura. Hindutva activists have already turned their attention to mosques in other towns. It is being said that Hindus have "woken up" after centuries of sleep. God forbid, if groups of Jains, Buddhists or Muslims were to emerge to agitate against their places of worship that were turned into Hindu temples. One fervently wishes that Jains and Buddhists are not "reawakend".

The official moves towards establishing a Hindu Rashtra have an external aspect. Such events are criticised by foreign media and send signals of religious intolerance in India. Modi's policies have justified the creation of a theocratic Pakistan. India keeps losing one battle of ideas after another. First by becoming a Hindu Pakistan and then by reshaping an ancient faith tradition as Abrahamic Hinduism!

Words of wisdom come from a villager in Haryana. He says what a scholar could have said: "Modiji, Hinduism continued to survive centuries of foreign rule because religion was not associated with the ruler. If it were associated with a Prime Minister or President or King, it would have died after his departure. So please keep it out of your politics!"

Courtesy: *The Wire*

Sectarian Hate has no Limits

The Bharatiya Janata Party (BJP) spokesperson Nupur Sharma's remarks about Prophet Muhammad in a TV debate shocked people of every faith. While the religious sensitivities of the Muslims were deeply hurt, the BJP kept quiet. Pliant journalists and social media legions were mobilised to defend Sharma. A meeting was organised in a temple in support of Nupur Sharma and the participants came armed with swords or were given swords there.

Prime Minister Narendra Modi, as usual, ignored the commotion but quickly realised it is one thing to target India's Muslims and another to provoke the wider Muslim world. When Qatar, and other Gulf nations conveyed their displeasure to Indian envoys or issued statements condemning the comments, it became clear that the BJP's domestic hate campaign was adversely affecting India's ties with the Islamic world were endangered. As the backlash threatened Indian exports to the region and the well-being of Indians working there, Modi realised he had to act. The BJP suspended Nupur Sharma from the party and expelled another leader, Naveen Jindal, for the same reason. Lofty rhetoric about respect for all religions was placed on record.

The BJP's action, taken under duress, is seen differently by different sections. Those concerned over the attacks and hate speeches directed against Muslims since Modi came to power in 2014 see these suspensions as a mere "damage-control" exercise. On their part, the Modi devotees are divided. Some clapped, convinced that one swallow does not make a summer. They hope to return to the business as usual, provoking Muslims with hate speeches and fuelling low-level conflict. Other devotees are angered by the BJP's action against their "heroine" who was doing a splendid job as the party's spokesperson. Their disappointment has filled social media. They say the BJP has let down the Hindus by buckling under pressure from Muslims. They feel Modi, whom they crowned as the 'Emperor of Hindu Hearts', has abandoned his mission. Hindus have been made orphans in their own land, screams one ideologue.

Of course, no one believes that the BJP's action against two of its leaders, taken on the pretext of inter-faith harmony, will promote the stated cause. Occasional tactical retreats have never deflected the ruling party from its polarisation mission designed to consolidate Hindu votes in its favour. The ruling party cannot afford to dilute its Hindutva ideology and stop projecting itself as the saviour of Hindus. So, this delayed gesture to placate public opinion in the Gulf countries lacks credibility.

The display of hostility towards Muslims by Sharma and other BJP and Sangh-oriented commentators on TV is part of a strategy to radicalise the minority community. Hindutva ideologues provoke to radicalise it. Hurting religious sentiments is the best weapon with which to provoke. The resulting anger and even violence by Muslims, if any, will help validate the BJP's campaign against the minority community.

Liberal Hindu commentators, deeply offended by Nupur Sharma's remarks, do not applaud the BJP's disciplinary action for another reason. The fact that the saffron party acted only after several Gulf countries protested the BJP leader's remarks sends a misleading message to the besieged Indian Muslims: That protection from persecution in their motherland will now come from the Islamic nations rather than from within India. This is problematic because the Gulf rulers are pragmatic and would like nothing more than to return to business as usual with India regardless of the BJP's policies. Nupur Sharma's 'clarification' – that she made offensive remarks about Islam because she felt Shiva was being insulted when the supposed *'shivaling'* at the Gyanvapi mosque was called a fountain – is a reminder of the distance Hinduism in India has travelled thanks to its use as a political instrument.

In the Sanatan Dharma tradition, questioning the 'supreme being' or criticising the various divine incarnations and manifestations is not unacceptable. Theological debates were encouraged in this faith tradition that has no central church, no religious head and no single definitive sacred book. Some years ago, before the empowerment of the Hindutva Brigade, a noted Hindi poetess could recite in public fora a poem criticising Lord Ram for his treatment of his wife. The Hindu audience enjoyed the poem.

This faith tradition produced a Tamil political leader who campaigned against the hegemony of Brahmins and the caste system and promoted social justice. He urged the people not to build temples. He called the ritual of dissolving the statue of Ganesh into water bodies a stupidity. In 1953, he bought a Ganesh statue and broke it. He urged the judge to also punish those who were immersing the idol in water on Ganesh Chaturthi. The judge released him. This leader, a social-activist fighting superstition and orthodoxy, had considerable political success. His name was E.V. Ramasamy.

All that changed with the empowerment of the Hindutva brigade. Those who are championing the closing of the Hindu mind will be only too happy with Muslims in India embracing a less moderate version of Islam. Against this backdrop, even the BJP's corrective step reflects the assertion of religion in politics and international affairs – a trend that is intrinsically dangerous. Multiple incidents of lynching and violence against Muslims did not cause so much anger as the offensive words against the Prophet. The Islamic countries were less perturbed by the threats of genocide against Muslims but protested effectively when the BJP spokesperson dragged the Prophet into the equation.

Religiosity matters, humanity does not. Indians grew up watching Hindi films that gave the message that humanity is above all. Take just one Bollywood song of those years written by a Muslim lyricist: *Na Hindu banega, na Musalman banega, tu insan ki aulad hai, insan banega.* That was the India that was.

Courtesy: The Wire

Communal India would harm Capitalists

Prime Minister Narendra Modi's use of money power has paid him a huge political dividend over the years. If the flood of funds continues, his disastrous anti-people decisions will extract no political price from him. Popular agitations against his Government, ignored by the pliant media, will be unable to strike hard enough. Mr Modi is carried by the corporate bigwigs over their shoulders, safely through the battleground of elections and choppy waters of mass unrest. The corporate power has become nearly invincible because of the astounding cost of elections. It is estimated to be more than Rs. 50,000 crores. Money makes democracy run. Some activists publicise the horrendous amounts spent on fighting elections. Most elected legislators and the Election Commission have no problem with such expenditure and the electoral reform groups' reports are consigned to the dustbin.

Modi shows his unlimited gratitude to the transparent and hidden donors by showering incentives on the private sector and selling to it the family silver, assets created by the public sector. This attracts more donors. Incentives are supplemented with vengeful official action which turns non-givers into eager contributors. Fear of the Government agencies makes the liberal donors shut the pipelines feeding the opposition parties. An opposition party starved of funds fails in electoral politics, notwithstanding its noble principles and ideological commitments. Pauperisation of his political opponents is what Mr Modi does so well.

Business leaders, incentivised or fearful, go through the regular routine of praising Mr Modi. They did so when he was the Chief Minister and do it even more when he is the Prime Minister. In another kind of country or in another time, such praise would have harmed a political leader depending on the masses who resent the rich. Neoliberal economic policies have altered the public image of the capitalist. To observe this change, one must watch the Bollywood movies of the fifties and sixties that portrayed him in an unfavourable light. Today's capitalists have the same traits but are seen differently. Modi's rise coincided with the emergence of the aspirational India. BJP's communalism should have hampered Modi in wooing the capitalists but Indian capitalists are generally short-sighted as they focus on short-term gains. They completely ignored the dangers of communalism and helped in its propagation even though most of them are not sectarian. Modi, who knows India's social fault lines better than an average academic, managed to yoke together the strange bedfellows – capitalism and communalism.

A test of the business leaders' humanity came in the context of the Gujarat communal killings in 2002. Gujarati captains of industry, who inherited the trusteeship principle, used to raise a voice against injustice and set an example for the rest to follow. They popularised a conciliatory approach to resolve differences and disputes. They never kept quiet in times of a disturbance. But in 2002, no more than one voice was raised. And soon even that fell silent perhaps because a signal from New Delhi.

The pattern was set. Big business learnt to be generous to Mr Modi and to seal its lips during any crisis affecting the common people. If a business leader happened to make an adverse comment against the Government, it made big news. Once Mr. Rahul Bajaj spoke up about rising intolerance in the presence of a union minister. That caused a lot of comments in the media that found it 'daring'!

On rare occasions, an eminent industrialist was unable to hold his tongue, ignoring the consequence. For example, Mr. Kishore Mariwala went public, saying how ashamed he was of India's reputation abroad. He shared on social media his experience in Phuket in Thailand where he had gone for a sailing holiday. He had charted a yacht and when he went to the company's office, the receptionist enquired if he was from India and if he was a Hindu. When he wondered why he was being asked this strange question, the receptionist replied: "Sir, all our skippers except one have gone with our other yachts. The only one left is a Muslim. I hope you don't mind that." A shell-shocked Mariwala said "not only I, but most cultured Hindus don't behave like this". Perhaps his prompt response was more effective than an Indian embassy press release about the 'fringe elements' of India.

The business tycoons saw Modi as their guide to a treasure island, not realising that communalism is not in their interest. They ought to value social harmony, if not on moral grounds, at least for pragmatic reasons. British history tells us that inter-religious clashes between the Catholics and Protestants declined sharply once the London Stock Exchange was established. This development was observed by Voltaire during his sojourn in England. He wrote that the people "lived happily together" because of the London Stock Exchange. "Go into the Exchange in London, that place more venerable than many a court, and you will see representatives of all the nations assembled there for the profit of mankind. There the Jew, the Mahometan and the Christian deal with one another as if they were of the same religion and reserve the name of infidel for those who go bankrupt." Commerce promotes tolerance and is promoted by tolerance.

A businessman should know that perennial social conflict fuelled by low-level religious violence is not good for business. Business needs social harmony to grow and prosper. While keeping the pot boiling through polarisation and identity politics wins votes for a party, it does not create a conducive investment climate. Even a small trader keeps his communal feelings under control while merrily selling goods to another community. Money has no colour of creed!

What happens to the business prospects of companies if a very large section is marginalised and its economic activity declines? What happens to economic growth and social progress when ordinary workers are unable to go to work and children are unable to go to school because of sustained low-level violence in vulnerable areas? The answers are easy to guess. Some business tycoons have quietly realised the danger, resulting in the flight of capital. They track the foreign investment trends and know why some international companies wound up their India operations recently. Some of them have bought property abroad just in case India keeps going in the wrong direction.

Examined from this angle, the Nupur Sharma episode illustrates how capitalism raised its voice against communalism. Without that the BJP spokesperson would have got away despite having hurt the religious feelings of Muslims by her comments on the Prophet. She had to be ultimately suspended, not because the Government was afraid of an agitation by Indian Muslims and not because some mighty western democracies issue statements advocating communal harmony in India. Here the tiny oil-rich nations proved more potent and influenced India's course of action in the Nupur Sharma case because a couple of prominent Indian business tycoons and the Government of India have strong business interests in the region where Islam is the dominant and official faith. Business overrode all considerations and Modi was forced to displease his core constituency that lionises Nupur Sharma. The Nupur Sharma episode dramatically conveyed to the Indian corporates that communalism does not pay.

And the political force that released the genie out of the bottle was not acting in their interests even though it appeared to be doing so by offering incentives at the cost of the national exchequer. But they helped in popularising the concept of a Hindu nation and now they cannot dethrone the Emperor of Hindu Hearts who has come to command mass following because of his wearing the religion on his sleeves and telling the majority to be fearful of a minority.

These rich tycoons can make some difference by distributing donations to political parties a bit equitably. That will weaken one of the pillars supporting the BJP's election machine. That will reduce the resources for horse-trading after every state election. If the BJP is not empowered with astronomical funds, its ability to polarise the electorate and promote identity politics will also be curtailed. What the Indian corporates do after discovering the dangers of communalism will be seen only at the time of the next parliamentary elections.

Courtesy: The Wire

Foreign Hand!

Some slogans never die. Sloganeers change. In Indian politics, those shouting "Foreign Hand! Foreign Hand!" today are different from those who shouted it during the cold war. Then, the Congress leaders used it, now the BJP leaders keep warning the nation that "the clawing foreign hand" is out to harm Prime Minister Narendra Modi and the nation. Foreign media organs, NGOs, civil rights activists, think tanks, Hinduism scholars, organisations monitoring freedom of expression and religious freedoms, and the rating agencies, are listed as the usual suspects.

A tweet storm was raised against the Opposition when US President Donald Trump publicly stated that millions of dollars of the USAID money was given to India for promoting voters' awareness. It was implied that the Opposition got the American money to upset Modi's apple cart. Then came Trump's next statement alleging that 21 million dollars of the USAID money was given to his "friend Modi". That stunned the BJP leaders and the trollers into silence. No BJP leader even asked America to stop interfering in India's internal affairs.

Ironically, the politico-cultural formation that brags about its genuine Indianness while promoting the Hindutva ideology, derived inspiration from Germany and Italy in their worst days. Its founders visited the two nations, liked their dictators, and admired their policies.

Social media is suffused with speculative comments that Trump has Modi's secrets which compels the Indian Prime Minister to follow whatever Trump says. That is why Trump is able to get from Modi whatever he wants to help the US economy. Old stories about the young Modi visiting the US for political training are retold. Questions are raised as to who paid for his extensive trip and training there and how he was groomed as a young political leader. The Indian Government of the day had made no fuss about young Modi's US visit since his training was for "strengthening democracy" in a developing country.

Modi's critics have urged the Prime Minister to respond to Trump's allegation. The Opposition has asked his Government to issue a White Paper on the USAID money coming to India. Of course, Modi's lips will remain sealed. Nothing will be officially clarified and the controversy will drag on and on to be finetuned for use in the next election campaign!

Modi's Intensive Trolling Cell had, in league with the Government and the Godi Media, attacked a foreign broadcasting company, a foreign multinational corporation, and an old American individual for conspiring against the Modi regime. The "foreign hand" had reached out from the evil West that breeds human right activists and anti-corruption crusaders. It guided one European NGO and an Australian journalist. It propelled a British university and a think tank. It made *The New York Times* and *The Guardian* sully Modi's image. The "foreign hand" pushed even Indians such as Rahul Gandhi to talk of press freedom and democracy during foreign visits. Modi's ministers and the BJP's army of trollers came out to crush the "foreign hand". The conspirators were "exposed" by paid trollers.

India's external affairs minister officially harped on this hot topic and surprised the US administration by his anti-west rhetoric. Looking at Modi's photo, it mumbled: You too Brutus? And that was all the US could do in the present geopolitical situation. After the decline of the non-aligned movement, the end of the cold war and a sharp spurt in India's economic growth, the West got over its animosity against India. It needs India to counter China and to benefit from its vast market.

This line taken by the western leaders is ignored by the NGOs of Europe and America. Two American institutions – Hindenburg and George Soros and the BBC of the UK strayed from the official line. The BBC released a documentary on the communal killings in Gujarat in 2002 when Narendra Modi was the chief minister. Hindenburg picked holes in the business of Modi's friend Adani. George Soros criticised Modi at the Munich Security Conference. He said the Indian Prime Minister would have to "answer questions" on the Adani controversy and the issue might weaken Modi's stranglehold on the Government. The pro-democracy sentiments expressed by Soros offended Modi's devotees. External Affairs Minister Jaishankar launched a personal attack on Soros calling him an "old, rich opinionated person" sitting in New York.

The west had not faced such vulgar attacks from India even during the heyday of the nonaligned movement. Jaishankar's pronouncements were suffused with a sharp anti-western rhetoric. He dusted off his inherited belief in nonalignment and understood Modi's commitment to self-alignment. He learnt from Modi that muscular diplomacy is needed for domestic politics. It is needed to strengthen muscular Hindutva. The external affairs minister's English speeches had the tone and tenor of the vernacular Hindu nationalists. India unleashed what noted commentator Avay Shukla calls "new werewolf warrior diplomacy".

Union minister and ex-TV actress Smriti Irani thundered that Soros had launched a war on India. What stands between the war and India's interests is Prime Minister Modi, she said. Irani assured the nation that India would defeat the foreign forces. Information and Broadcasting Minister Anurag Thakur slammed *The New York Times* and a few like-minded foreign media organs for spreading lies about India and Prime Minister Narendra Modi. Indians would not allow such an agenda on Indian soil, he announced. The genteel official spokesman described the BBC documentary as a conspiracy against India. Social media called the BBC names. The Government banned the documentary and the income tax officers raided the BBC offices in Delhi and Mumbai.

The "foreign hand" did not feel daunted. It "enticed" the Opposition leader Rahul Gandhi to do its bidding! He was invited to the UK where he gave lectures on the decline of democracy in Modi's India. For days, the BJP leaders called for stringiest action against Rahul Gandhi for committing a crime on a foreign land! The Congress hit back by unearthing and showing several old videos of Modi debunking the Congress-ruled India during his foreign trips.

During the Emergency imposed by Indira Gandhi, those belonging to the BJP's parental organisation used to go abroad, to "defame" their nation and seek foreign help in fighting the Congress rule. In fact, when Mrs Gandhi came back to power, Bruno Kreisky admitted to her that as

Austria's Chancellor, he did help an Indian opposition leader in his campaign against her during the Emergency.

The "evil foreign hand" has been Modi's weapon of choice during the poll campaigns. Modi uses it to manufacture mass outrage and portray the Opposition as "anti-national". The master strategist perfected the formula by launching a tirade against "Mia Musharraf" to win a state assembly election! Modi managed to be seen as the knight in shining armour, out to defeat the conspiracy to destabilise India. So, Hindenburg, Soros, and the BBC served the ruling BJP's purpose.

Modi is not afraid of bad publicity. A strong leader needs an enemy. Constant shadow boxing keeps the people impressed by performance politics. In 2002, the people of Gujarat saw Modi defeating an "internal enemy" and crowned him as the "Emperor of Hindu Hearts", showering him with votes, more valuable than rose petals. The BJP then projected Modi as a target of the "anti-national forces" in the country.

Those defending the current use of the "foreign hand" in domestic politics say that Indira Gandhi also talked about it. They ignore that the west's relationship with India was then openly hostile. It disapproved of the nonaligned moment and India's close relations with the Soviet Union. Indira Gandhi's independent foreign policy was an anathema to the West. An American President, who hated Indira Gandhi, used an expletive for her. The anti-Indira movement run by the opposition leaders did get foreign help. America's anti-Indian role during the Bangladesh war was no secret. Britain denied help to India during the Indo-Pakistan war. In Britain, in the eighties, the Khalistani outfit and the Jammu and Kashmir Liberation Front agitating against India, used to get a friendly signal from official agencies. When a Khalistani leader, appearing in a TV programme, threatened to kill the Indian Prime Minister, the British Government said it is committed to the principle of freedom of speech.

That was when the cold war was on, the CIA was acting to destabilise India and Indira Gandhi, the strong independent leader, faced America's animosity. Now the US is the strategic partner of India that has opened its market and adopted the American approach towards Muslims. During those years, alerts against the "foreign hand" made sense. Now the western powers led by America are very friendly which has diminished the CIA's role in India. After 9/11, the west began to see the human rights issue differently. Earlier, the killing of a single Kashmiri Muslim by the security forces used to shock British Parliament and the US Congress. Now, Junaids get lynched or burnt in India without getting noticed by any western leader. Modi was lucky to come to power when he did. After 9/11, anyone spreading Islamophobia is encouraged by the west that itself took to killing the people in the Islamic nations.

This hypocrisy in overlooking the atrocities against Muslims in India and the state's violation of the civil rights have not gone unnoticed by western journals. They criticised their leaders' silence over the killings of Muslims in India and the ban on the BBC documentary. An *Economist* columnist said: "The next time Banyan hears a western leader congratulating Mr. Modi on their countries' "shared democratic values", his stomach will turn."

Foreign Mouth!

Rihanna of America opened her mouth in support of the agitating farmers of India. She tweeted: "Why are we not talking to the protesting farmers". The Modi devotees saw a fresh foreign conspiracy against India! In the context of the farmers' agitation, the case of 20 ex-IFS officers was more curious. Agriculture was not an area of their expertise and yet they entered the fray by opposing the farmers' agitation and supporting the Modi Government's farm laws. With Rihanna trying to rock Modi's boat, they saw years of their public diplomacy effort wasted. The ex-ambassadors were informed by their daughters that Rihanna is a pop singer with a record global following.

The developed countries wanted India to reform its agriculture so they must restrain Rihanna. The ex-IFS officers issued a statement warning these countries "not to be on the wrong side of the history". As if those who write history will heed such a warning. Some ex-ambassadors perhaps discussed how Rihanna could be made to sing a song in praise of Modi.

India's far-sighted Prime Minister fraternised with the heads of American social media corporations and yet they did not freeze Rihanna's twitter account. Nor did the US Government tell Rihanna to keep quiet about India's farmers. Rihanna is unlike the Indian celebrities who tweet the dictated tweet in support of the Government. Meryl Streep condemned the U S President at the prestigious platform of Golden Globes. She got a loud applause from the distinguished audience. Arundhati Roy was applauded when she assailed the U S Administration at a meeting in New York. Let her do that to the Indian Government and see the results.

The retired IFS officers are divided. The 'concerned' retired officers criticise the Government. As many as 99 retired officers of three premier all-India services asked the Government not to assault civil liberties, freedom of speech and the right to dissent. What they did not want the Government to do, it started doing even more vigorously. So, it became more dangerous to urge the Government to allow dissent.

Modi Kal, sold to public as *Amrit Kal* has seen a sharp division among faiths and within every faith. Most families are divided over the idea of India. The ideological turbulence caused by Prime Minister Narendra Modi has not spared even sacred institutions such as universities. Most institutions have been divided and now function under new heads planted by the regime. One sees spectacles like a Nehru Association organising a seminar on *Manusmriti* and a Gandhi Sanstha celebrating the Savarkar Jayanti! Oddly, the regime change influenced even a section of Nehru's children and grandchildren who had spent years basking in the glory of the Nehruvian ethos. Imagine a section of the former IITians supporting the anti-scientific temper lobby through social media posts. Imagine the former members of the hallowed Indian Foreign Service (IFS) falling for an anti-Nehru mofussil political leader. So, it was a bit of a surprise when 20 ex-IFS officers came out in support of the controversial farm laws. Film actors and cricketers took to twitter to help the regime. The 20 ex-IFS officers also heard

Modi's call and joined the IAF (India Against Farmers) campaign. What have the IFS officers to do with farming? They know the fine distinction between German and Italian wines but cannot distinguish between wheat and rapeseed crops. They jumped into the fray because they believed that the current crisis was not about farming but about India's image sullied by the farmers.

The protesting farmers tackled barbed wire and steel spikes but could not cope with this onslaught. They were unable to read the English statement by experts in drafting papers and non-papers. The farmers produced no IFS officer and thus could not get help from their kith and kin. Farmers used to be hailed as givers of daily bread but got deleted from the Jai Jawan, Jai Kisan slogan once they made India surplus in food grains. Had India been still living from ship-to-mouth, no government would have dared to ignore farmers. They used to burden only their families by committing suicide or occasionally the police and jail authorities. Now they created a problem for diplomats. And that too in the wake of the Prime Minister's triumphant tour of the US which demonstrated that as an emerging Superpower, India can meddle into America's domestic politics.

Some former officers also began to express their reservations about India's ethical foreign policy that they considered to be a contradiction in terms. They understood diplomacy as a patriotic art of lying for one's country and welcomed New India's muscular diplomacy. Their colleagues in service meekly accepted the new dominant role of the TV anchors in making India's foreign policy laced with hyper nationalism. These anchors emerged as interlocutors between the Prime Minister and the Ministry of External Affairs.

The IFS has been traditionally free of dissent. If foreign policy is distorted and deployed to serve domestic politics, no officer gets stricken by conscience and resigns. Quite unlike the American diplomat in Dhaka who quit the service because he disagreed with America's pro-Pak policy during the Bangladesh conflict. IFS is a disciplined service. It follows the golden rule of following the Prime Minister of the day. After all, foreign policy has always been the Prime Minister's special domain. So, when the new regime came, they started drafting a new kind of papers and delegated two of their clan to the Union Cabinet which could not depend entirely on the RSS *pracharaks*-turned ministers.

Tracking the wind's new direction, they supported moves to intensify strategic partnership with the U S, giving an indecent burial to the Non-Aligned Movement. They knew some BJP leaders had wanted to send Indian troops to Iraq when the then US President asked India to join the coalition of the willing. However, the then BJP Prime Minister disagreed with his colleagues and did not let Indian blood be shed in a distant battlefield. That BJP Prime Minister is no more and some leaders will be glad to let India be America's Subedar-Major since the US is letting two Indian multinationals prosper.

An internal study says if India joins the US camp, an elected dictator can safely run the country without facing any criticism from the White House. It lists the privileges that Pakistan enjoyed as a follower of the US. The ex-IFS officers perhaps blame their senior colleagues for ignoring the reality of the post-cold war world. However, in drafting the statement in support of the farm laws, they also show their upbringing in the Nehruvian ethos. So, they did not hesitate from exposing the perfidy of the powerful West influencing

India's domestic economic policies by using the WTO to limit India's sovereignty. Some formulations from their old drafts against WTO crept into the statement. They said, "the WTO agreement on agriculture was characterised by democratic deficit and based on commercial realpolitik".

They made appropriate references to "developing countries" but went on to offer a carrot to the crafty developed nations by promising that "India will gradually and incrementally allow the market to decide prices of agricultural produce". The U S leaders love the word 'market'. They sent a reassuring signal to the monopolist corporations of America and India eying India's agri-business for long. So, their statement is a mix of the old and new. They said the developed countries "can't have your cake and eat it too". The insinuation was justified because this gang of developed countries forces India to 'reform' agriculture and then when it undertakes reforms, it does not protect the Government of India from the angry activists. These governments fail to discipline their media, pop singers and activists and prevent them from poking their noses into India's internal affairs. Why did they allow their activists to ask the Government of India to talk to the farmers? Why were they letting their TV channels report that farmers were denied water, electricity, and internet facility? Why were these showing images of barbed-wire-steel-nail fencing confining the protesting farmers. The statement by implication highlighted the hypocrisy of the developed countries.

Protecting India's image is crucial. The Government should use these 20 ex-IFS officers for this noble mission. An IFS officer never retires. He is ready to sacrifice his well-earned leisure and Black-Labelled-liquid-soaked evenings to serve as a Union Minister. So, the Government should appoint these signatories to the statement as ambassadors-at-large and direct them to visit different nations to counter the propaganda by Rihanna and a Swedish girl. A high-level committee including Bollywood stars and cricketers should be formed. An American PR agency that worked for an election campaign in India should be engaged. The Sadanand Foundation be given a grant of Rs 30 crores to run this "Indians for India's Image" project. These officers be made fellows of the foundation so that a change of regime does not affect their careers. Before beginning their work abroad, the ex-officers should be taken on a tour of the ancient centres of India's civilisation so that they highlight the democratic principles enshrined in sacred Hindu texts and the glory that was India!

Pluralism united Hindus
Hindutva divides Hindus

The impact of Hindutva on national politics and society is analysed extensively but religious scholars have not discussed much about what Hindutva is doing to Hinduism. And even less is said about the so-called defenders and promoters of muscular Hinduism making the community fearful and less self-confident. What kept Hindus more united as compared to the followers of the Abrahamic faith traditions is the pluralism enshrined in Hinduism. The right to contest any theological principle and to publicly disagree with a sacred text or a preacher is what gave Hinduism its strength and resilience. An atheist can rightfully be a Hindu. He cannot be charged with blasphemy for doubting God. Even a devout Hindu can question God. *Nasadiya Sukta* of the *Rig Veda* wonders whether even the creator of the universe, is omniscient! Expression of this view in a Vedic hymn never hurt the Hindu psyche. The Hindutva Hindus know almost nothing about Hinduism. They want to follow Islam and Christianity by adopting the concept of blasphemy in this more sophisticated and noble faith tradition. The violent intra-faith conflicts in Christianity or Islam can be largely attributed to rigidity and orthodoxy. That kind of rigidity and uniformity is sought to be injected by the BJP into Hinduism to make it muscular! The drive towards uniformity can only make identity politics stronger.

The political movement of Hindutva spearheaded by those wanting to unite Hindus, has divided Hindus. Ironically, the Hindutva lobby that asks Hindus to be proud, makes Hindus less self-confident and fearful of imagined assaults by "the other". By their campaign, the BJP and its fringe organisations have dented the self-confidence of the Hindu community.

Scholar Ashis Nandy says sources of Hindutva are no different than those of Islam. The Hindutva activists see Hinduism as inferior to the masculine, monolithic, well-organised Semitic creeds. Hinduism and Hindutva will confront each other in a struggle unto death, says Prof. Nandy. For the RSS, the ideal Indian is the brown-skinned version of the colonial police sergeant, reading the Gita instead of the Bible. Hindutva is Western imperialism's last frenzied kick at Hinduism. He does not believe Hindutva will be the end of Hinduism. Hinduism has dealt with such pathologies affecting faith for long and it will deal with one more, Prof. Nandy says.

How Indian politics fares under the spell of Hinduism is covered extensively by the media. It is time scholars such as Karen Armstrong, studying religions, wrote on the impact of contemporary politics on Hinduism. Can this unique religion be modified by politicians aided by frenzied devotees in India and the Hollywood Hindus of America? A noble faith tradition, hijacked for political purposes, is getting vulgarised. One would have expected Hindu saints to rise and guide Hindus and warn them against the conspiracy by political leaders to exploit religion. The use of religion in politics is criticised by secular politicians but respected religious scholars and heads of genuine spiritual institutions keep quiet. Surely, they must be pained by the slow degradation of their faith. Islamic scholars are blamed for not condemning the misuse of their faith by politicians or terrorists. The situation is no different in the context of Hinduism. One may ask: where have the real spiritual seekers gone? There have been a few exceptions. Long before communalism acquired this virulent a form, Swami Ranganathananda, an eminent monk, warned against mixing religion with politics. The President of the Ramakrishna Mission, who died in 2005, said in an interview that communal parties should have been banned in a secular State. "It should be done now for the good of both religion and politics. Religion goes down because politics is played by politicians with violence, falsehood, and trickery. Religion must be retrieved from such a situation. Let religions function with harmony, peace, and humanistic attributes, then our politics will become better. The passion and the frenzy that religion inducts into politics will not be there. Silent and steady politics will come when we have the separation of religion from secular political activities", he said.

India has gone in the opposite direction, especially after Modi, an RSS functionary, emerged on the political scene. There has been an outbreak of faux religiosity as political devotees of Modi began to propagate muscular Hinduism. They are assembled at events where the *sarkari* (pro-Government) "seers" bless the ruling party. The seers want political patronage; the ruling party needs their endorsement. The diversity and tolerance of Hinduism enabled the establishment of a secular state even in the wake of horrendous sectarian violence of the Partition. Then the parent bodies of today's *Hindutva* forces failed to politically challenge Nehru and Nehruvian ethos. That was the India that was!

Terms such as "Hindu Terror" or "Hindu Taliban" have emerged in the recent years. The rise of *Hindutva* forces has made many Hindus anxious. A few of them left this faith to protest its vulgarisation. Hindus of a certain class are more comfortable practicing a Japanese school of Buddhism. In the mid 15th century, Guru Nanak Dev, a born Hindu, rebelled against impurities in this faith and exploitation by its priestly class. His teachings led to the foundation of Sikhism. More than 60 years ago, eminent Dalit leader B. R. Ambedkar converted to Buddhism, taking with him thousands of Hindus belonging to his oppressed caste. Ambedkar condemned the caste system and even said, "If Hindu Raj does become a fact, it will, no doubt be the greatest calamity for this country." To woo the

Dalit voters, the BJP leaders today pay rich tributes to this very leader, ignoring his attacks on Hinduism. Appropriation through misrepresentation is what the BJP does best!

Hindutva seeks to stop argumentation, contestation, and inquiry but ironically it has made more Hindus, including the westernised ones, to explore mythology, history and principles associated with Hinduism. So many learned articles on these topics would not have been written but for Modi trying to push India on to the Hindutva path. Even fiction is written and read in this context.

Shorn of its inclusiveness and laced with bigotry, Hinduism will threaten not just the religious minorities but a very large section of practicing Hindus. In the neighbouring theocratic state of Pakistan, non-Sunni sections of Muslims have always felt threatened.

Hinduism has millions of gods and goddesses worshipped in a hundred different ways. Hinduism sanctifies sacrifices of the Vedic Aryans as well as the rituals of primitive tribes. A sacred text features *Mahadevi,* the Great Goddess who encompasses the thousands of local and regional *devis* as well as the pan-Indian goddesses. This most democratic religion presided over by a Parliament of Gods had no founder and is without one single authoritative book. Hindus continue to worship Gods both in iconic and aniconic forms. And not only are there numerous gods and goddesses but even a single god or goddess appears in several forms. Hindus of one region in India may accord primacy to one form while of another region may not worship that form at all. Within the fold of this faith, each one acts according to his individual belief. There is no one single prescribed common form of worship. One may try to reach God through work, or meditation and knowledge or simply through devotion. Each way is as valid as every other. India's philosopher-President Radhakrishnan said what counts is conduct, not belief. That is why Hinduism embraces believers and non-believers, the theist and the atheist, the sceptic and the agonistic.

Scholar Kshiti Mohan Sen writes that the uniting force among the enormous variety of religious beliefs and ceremonies in Hinduism has been a belief in a basic code of behaviour. The recent years have witnessed some Hindu groups indulging in an un-Hindu-like conduct under political compulsions. The lynching of alleged beef transporters is a recent example. The belief-driven chariot that reached Ayodhya in 1992 led not only to the destruction of a place of worship but also to killings.

Hindutva, a political form of faith propagated by the ruling BJP and allied Right-wing groups, has been injected with full force into the election campaigns. Hindu gods are made to descend on the political battle-field. The movement for building a Ram temple on a disputed plot of land where a mosque stood before its demolition in 1992, ended with the triumph for the Hindutva votaries. At times, the *Hindutva* card does not give desired election results but misrepresentation of the true spirit of Hinduism does not cease.

The BJP sets the terms of political discourse dominated by the Ram temple, women's entry into a temple, castes and sub-castes, and protection of the holy cow. A mob agitating against alleged cow slaughter kills two persons including a police officer in a BJP-ruled State that has a monk as it chief minister. Yogi Adityanath campaigns for the party, inciting communal hatred to consolidate Hindu votes.

At times, such statements misfire. A statement made to garner the Dalit votes caused a blowback that the Yogi had not imagined. The Yogi told an election rally that Lord Hanuman, known as Monkey God in the West, was a Dalit (belonging to an oppressed caste). Dalit leaders demanded that since Hanuman was a Dalit, all Hanuman temples should have Dalit priests, and these and the offerings should be handed over to them! The Dalits took their protests to temples and in one, the Brahmin priest was forced to leave the building. A woman Dalit parliamentarian resigned from the ruling BJP saying that Lord Hanuman faced humiliation because he happened to be a Dalit. He helped Lord Ram win the war against the demon king, Ravan, and yet he was turned into a monkey with a black face!

The Yogi also offended the Brahmins, the priestly class, who were not amused by his calling Hanuman a Dalit. Some protesting Brahmins filed a legal case against the Yogi. One leader in the Yogi's own party said Hanuman was not a Dalit but an Arya since the caste system had not started in his age! This will be contested by those who worship Ram as a *Kshatriya* (belonging to the warrior caste). In fact, there is a pro-BJP royal Rajput family that claims to have descended from the family of Lord Ram!

A non-Brahmin monk, who runs a mega business and supports the ruling BJP, invoked the sacred texts saying that caste is determined not by birth but by the nature of duties performed by a Hindu. Since Hanuman burnt down Sri Lanka to make Ram victorious in his war against Ravan, he was a *Kshatriya*! In New India, things do get weird at times. The amused secular Hindus grumble that after dividing humans for political gains, the BJP is now dividing Gods based on caste! Commenting on this strange political discourse, many lament that the election campaigns do not focus on the livelihood issues. Foreign observers wondered what exotic Indians are talking about and what do they really want from an elected government?

With the ruling BJP repeatedly playing the *Hindutva* card in elections, sectarian violence have become the new normal. It creates emotional frenzy through a divisive rhetoric, mythological tales and warnings of the danger posed by the religious "Other". Politicians shun theological complexities and the tradition of disputation and argumentation in Hinduism. They use mythology to convey a simplified common version of the faith. Since there is no single central creed, political campaigners can pick and choose a religious saying to validate their assertion suited to the audience they are addressing. The ruling party leaders want the people to feel, not to think. They propagate modified Hinduism, devoid of its flexibility, inclusiveness, diversity, tolerance, and other liberal features. They make statements to incite the conservatives.

The BJP Government undertook to reform Islam by outlawing an unfair divorce process victimising Muslim women. But reformation of Hinduism is a no-go area. In fact, progressive Hindus and a law court seeking the latter provoked the BJP which organised protests when the Supreme Court ruled that woman of all ages should be allowed entry in a south Indian Hindu temple! The BJP President asked courts to pass only such judgments that are "implementable" and refrain from hurting the Hindu sentiments.

Politicians using religion advocate economic reforms but oppose religious reforms. Hindus hesitate to talk of reforms lest they are called anti-Hindu. Political mobs are unleashed on the reformists who fight bigotry and assert the inclusiveness of Hinduism. Swami Agnivesh, an advocate of the Vedic tradition and a social activist, faced physical assaults. Orthodoxy is encouraged. Atrocious statements are issued. A poll candidate said if she is elected, the police will not be allowed to check child marriage! The atmosphere reeks of bigotry and hostility towards other faiths keeps growing. Children learn that when we say prayers loudly, it is worship, when they worship loudly, it is disturbing noise!

Politicisation retards reforms needed by every faith that accumulates undesirable rituals. Hinduism, being a product of many cultures and cults, is more prone to do so. In its long journey, Hinduism acquired and discarded many questionable rituals. Some religious practices were abolished in response to the challenge posed by Christianity. Commenting on this process of reforms and renewal, scholar Kshiti Mohan Sen writes that the impact of the West produced new schools of thought which emphasised old doctrines.

Hinduism has a history of reforms. Swami Dayanand Saraswati (1824-83), who founded the *Arya Samaj*, gave the call "Back to the *Vedas*", drawing a large section of Hindus away from idol-worship and exploitative priests. *Arya Samaj* established educational institutions and worked to raise the status of the backward classes. It introduced proselytization, which was no part of the Hindu traditions. Swami Dayanand came from the State of Modi who used regional pride as an electoral card. Curiously, videos glorify the sons of Gujarat barring the *Arya Samaj* founder! Praising this great Gujarati will pose a problem for the BJP that made the Ram temple a central issue of its political campaign. *Arya Samaj* opposes idol-worship. The Vedic tradition involved sacred sacrifice in the open. The Indo-Aryans did not build permanent structures for the practice of their religion. Temples began to be built much later when worship and supplication were added to sacrifice in the Hindu religious ethos.

In Bengal, Raja Rammohun Roy (1774-1833) founded the *Brahmo Samaj* facing opposition by orthodox Hindus who were against his progressive outlook on social matters. He advocated modern education and wanted Indians to learn science and technology. His agitation led to the abolition of the criminal practice of *Sati* that ordained a wife to commit suicide by plunging into the fire consuming her dead husband. Another new school of Hinduism developed in Bengal under the influence of Ramakrishna Paramhamsa (1834-86) that appealed to the common man who just prays before a deity without bothering about theology. This simple communication with God became very popular and came to be known as the *Bhakti* movement. There were reformers in south India and other parts of the country who are venerated till today. They have left behind institutions that attract many followers.

In British India, conservative Hindu leaders debated with reformers vigorously, but that contestation was due to clashing beliefs and not a political strategy for use in a democracy. Today conservative Hindu leaders are glad to be corralled into supporting Prime Minister Modi. The frequently organised massive gatherings of Hindu monks in saffron are politically valuable for the BJP! The BJP strategists have a vested interest in the Hinduism of communal ceremonies and public rituals that make good TV and help political campaigning on the religious platform.

Secular politicians distinguish between Hinduism and BJP's *Hindutva* to highlight the inclusive nature of the genuine faith that assimilated principles from many cultures during its 5000 years of history. Not all Hindu gods are Aryan gods. The secular politicians reason well but they cannot influence those waving the saffron flags, shouting slogans and throwing bricks.

Leftists, not well-versed in India's cultural traditions, have little leverage as the faithful do not belong to their constituency. Only firm believers, who protest the "hijacking of our religion", can make convincing counter arguments. They alone can increase public understanding of Hinduism unsullied by politics. The sacred texts of Hinduism never encourage bigotry. In the wake of the demolition of the Ayodhya mosque, Prof. Amartya Sen said fanaticism grew mainly because neglecting classics in education. Anand Patwardhan, noted documentary maker, says the TV serial, *Ramayan,* watched by millions, paved the way for the demolition of the Babri mosque. "A bow-and-arrow bearing Ram entered every household and every heart." Television too popularises pop religion to cause social disharmony. Those rushing to break a mosque or place an idol on a disputed plot of land, all in the name of Hinduism, know nothing about a faith that had no founder and that assimilated various religions as well as cultural movements. They are familiar with folklore, mythology, and stories of miracles but unaware of the Vedic *Song of Creation* that wonders whether even the Creator knows all! That questioning will be considered blasphemy in other religions.

In fact, media erroneously used the term Hindu fundamentalists to describe the political leaders such as L. K. Advani when he went to Ayodhya in a chariot to demand the building of a temple to Lord Ram. That movement resulted in the destruction of a mosque. Advani, knowing that the term fundamentalism had acquired a bad odour in the context of Islam, hastened to declare that they were Hindu nationalists and not fundamentalists. He was correct because going back to the fundamentals in his religion would mean the Vedic tradition that will rob the proposed Ram temple of all significance! Advani's 1992 movement to build a Ram temple on the plot where the mosque stood generated a toxic mix of religion and nationalism turned into a potent political weapon.

Respect for religions is a principle enshrined in India's Constitution. Religious polarisation diminishes the

Constitution and democracy. Hinduism is diminished by screams that faith is bigger than the Constitution! When a BJP chief minister plans to build the biggest statue of Lord Ram, the state gives a crass dimension to idol-worship. When a secular chief minister tells her political enemies using Lord Ram in electoral battles that she has the protection of Goddess Durga, she conjures up a silly competition between the two, showing disrespect to both. Display of faux religiosity and ritual are getting more popular. TV programmes draw heavily on mythology and cover religious events more extensively.

Resistance to reforms reinforces orthodoxy that carries great emotional appeal. The influence of the *Arya Samaj* has declined. Anecdotal evidence suggests that the numbers of Hindus going to temples and Muslims going to mosques have increased. The nexus of politics and religion has resulted in the proliferation of *Ashrams* and *Babas*. Assured of official protection in lieu of their vote delivering powers, charlatans established institutions attracting many devotees. Some of them have been exposed as criminals. Consequently, the word *Ashram* has been devalued. To make Hinduism muscular, the BJP fuels intolerance and competitive sectarianism. An atmosphere is created in which religious sentiments get hurt even by a stray comment or a video. Hardly a week goes by without a political activist shouting in a TV studio that Hindu sensitivities have been hurt by some statement or the other. The 'hurt' Hindu psyche leads to a militant response through street violence and denunciation of the rival faith. A reference to the women playmates of Lord Krishna provokes an educated Hindu political activist to write a long post on the Christian women who consider themselves married to Jesus!

Many Hindus living outside India actively 'protect' their gods and goddesses from insults. Hollywood Hindus ignore that their faith felt strong enough to allow internal theological differences and dissent. It neutralised competing elements by absorbing them. Hindus felt confident enough to ignore silly remarks against their faith. But politicians find heightened sensitivities useful for rallying forces against the religious 'Other'.

Hinduism is not the product of a major revelation granted to a prophet. Had Hinduism been different, it would not have permitted a monk to become a politician and there would be no Yogi-Chief Minister. By decrying secularism, some politicians want India to imitate Pakistan. By modifying Hinduism, they want it to imitate Islam, a religion of the Book.

Thanks to the inherent strength and resilience of Hinduism, the powerful impact of the West did not lead to large-scale conversions to Christianity. In fact, the British rulers kept away from reforms in Hinduism some of which seeking gender parity and social justice were undertaken by the Government of independent

India. Foreign rulers posed little danger to Hinduism but if one were to believe the Hindu nationalists, today 70 years after India's independence, Hinduism is in danger! This slogan is designed to make the majority fearful and to promote hatred towards the religious 'Other'. Votaries of Political Hinduism would like to adopt an absolute central creed so that Hindus claim that their view is the only view. The warning of "Hinduism in danger", seers blessing the BJP at election time and violent protests by Hindutva activists mark political contestation. At times faith sways voters but at times it yields no political dividends. Many Hindutva rally participants are hired, given saffron head-bands, told to shout a particular slogan, and brought to the venue by buses.

At times, the *Hindutva* forces face a setback but it is not caused by any revulsion against the politics of hatred and the misuse of Hinduism. The Hindus given to bowing their heads while passing by a mosque or a church are in a majority, but it is a silent majority. Such Hindus grieve privately when their liberal faith is violated while the public fora is left free for the *Hindutva* votaries. Those Hindus who, like devout Muslims, felt pained by the demolition of the Babri mosque in Ayodhya, did not come out on the streets to do penance as Gandhi would have done. They did not challenge the Hindu activists celebrating the mosque demolition anniversary on December 6 as a day of bravery. So, the voices of liberal Hindus remain unheard. Their presence gets noticed only when they are physically attacked by the Hindutva brigade.

Here is a stray example of the typical reaction of genuine devout Hindus to the destruction of the Babri mosque. The elderly Gujarati mother of writer Salil Tripathi on watching the mosque destruction on the TV rang her son in Singapore. She said on phone: "We have just killed Gandhi again." She added: *Avu te karaay koi divas?* (in Prime Minister Narendra Modi's mother tongue). Can anyone do such a thing any time? Her statement comes closest to what is said in gentle Britain: Simply not done!

After the BJP came to power in 2014, there has been a phenomenal rise of believers in the aggressive political *Hindutva* as also in the numbers of the RSS volunteers. Digital warriors go after anyone talking about the philosophical dimension of this inclusive, eclectic, and dialogic faith. Anyone citing the sacred texts, be he a Hindu Sanskrit pundit or a scholar proficient in English, is branded anti-Hindu and "sickular". Social media is suffused with tirades against such Hindus. Their posts reflect their lack of familiarity with modern languages and classical literature, let apart books on theology and philosophy.

The refrain is the same. Hinduism is in danger and it must appear in an aggressive avatar. The *Hindutva* votaries say that because of the gentle nature of their religion Hindus were victimised in the past. It appears as if India has just got free from the Islamic rulers and now Hindu warriors are out to protect Hinduism from depredations by a foreign faith. If historians depend on the media to collect the spoken and written words, they will find that political *Hindutva* became extremely popular during this period.

Many devout Hindus are shocked by the politicisation of their faith and attempts to impose a cruel muscular creed. But faced with organised mob frenzy, they surrender to silence. All they can do is to write letters to the editor. On the anniversary of the mosque demolition, a letter written by a Hindu refers to "India's darkest hour and a huge blow to our multi-cultural identity". Another letter condemns the latest killings associated with alleged cow slaughter. It suggests that one can get away with much in the name of religion. "How can anger and violence become expressions of religious fervour?"

Such voices are hardly heard when thousands of men in saffron electrify a mass rally, demanding the building of temples by demolishing mosques! The situation can be changed only if a fearless devout Hindu reformer emerges to free Hinduism from the clutches of politicians and to detoxify society through a cultural revolution. He or she should be able to influence a community's social psychology. Some seers may then start spreading the true message of Hinduism. Secularism must influence consciousness and shape social and political imagination. It had done so even during the more challenging times of the post-Partition communal killings. That will make it difficult to mobilise mobs against the Hindus not subscribing to *Hindutva* and against court rulings that seek to loosen the hold of religious orthodoxy.

The *Hindutva* forces do face hurdles in uniting Hindus on one single political platform. Varied and pluralistic traits of Hinduism resist uniformity. Hindus believe in the existence of many ways of reaching God. All sacred texts and hymns emphasise this. The BJP's campaign to establish the primacy of Lord Ram cannot succeed in large parts of the country where people cherish their own devotional ethos. They will not start establishing Ram temples at the behest of a political formation. In fact, they resent attempts to violate their patterns of belief. A BJP Minister's idea of giving a special formal status to the *Bhagavad Gita* just fizzled out. In some States, the BJP cannot afford to launch its aggressive campaign against beef-eating.

The diversity within the faith makes it difficult to impose uniformity. Notwithstanding the infiltration of the Right-wing Hindu activists in several official and autonomous institutions, the conversion of India into a theocratic state will remain a dream of the BJP-RSS combine.

How far the politicians will succeed in their polarisation project? The BJP's rule in New Delhi and several States enables it to popularise *Hindutva* but if the BJP loses political power, it will find it impossible tp achieve its goal. That is why winning elections has become for it a matter of supreme importance and the BJP leaders fight poll battles with messianic zeal. In fact, retaining power is critical for them because their vigilante groups would face public fury once the BJP is out of power.

Events will be planned and demands will be made for demolishing more mosques. This strategy makes the BJP confident of winning. The Prime Minister declares that he would cleanse the country of its main Opposition! The *Hindutva* forces continue their mission to capture political power to establish a Hindu Nation. Their progress since the demolition of the Babri mosque indicates that they are not going to disappear anytime soon. No atonement is expected from the forces that stoked the sectarian fire.

Politicians will tinker with Hinduism, but can they modify Hinduism or change the way Hindus look at their religion? Many believe the current aberration shall pass. They say Hinduism withstood challenges by foreign rulers of alien faiths. It can withstand attacks by *desi* politicians. The distance between religion and state may widen again. Diversity may strengthen the inclusive character of Hinduism. Private contemplation may become attractive. The new fad of communal well-publicised idol-worship may subside a little. They believe once the pitcher of sins fills up to the brim, the Divine intervenes to set the creation right again! They have the word of Lord Krishna in the *Bhagavad Gita*:

> *Whenever there is decay of*
> *Righteousness, O Bharata,*
> *And there is exaltation of*
> *Unrighteousness, then I Myself*
> *Come forth, for the protection*
> *of the good, for the destruction*
> *of evil-doors, for the sake of*
> *firmly establishing Righteousness,*
> *I am born from Age to age.*

> (Translated by Swami Vivekananda)

Goodbye, Gandhi!

October 2 was the best day for Mahatma Gandhi, it was the worst day for Mahatma Gandhi. The President, Prime Minister, Governors, and Chief Ministers paid tributes to Gandhi's memory; some Hindu nationalists took to social media to pay tributes to Gandhi's killer. Thousands garlanded Gandhi's statues; a few saffron-clad Hindus garlanded his killer's statue. The world celebrated Mahatma Gandhi's birth anniversary as Nonviolence Day; some countries marked the day by violent deeds. In India, the day saw police action against poor farmers trying to enter Delhi to highlight their plight. Indian political leaders read out homilies but they sucked morality out of politics. They called on the nation to follow the Gandhian path while their governments promoted economic policies that went against Gandhi's vision.

In seminars and TV studios, some said Gandhi was more relevant today, some others said Gandhi was outdated in the modern age. Gandhi placed the poorest of the poor in the company of God by calling him *Daridra Narayan*. Today's political leaders talk about the poor during the election campaigns, but once in power help the rich accumulate more wealth.

Gandhi has been forgotten by those who oppress the lower castes and women, deliver hate speeches against a minority, and indulge in violence. Such incidents have increased and what is more vicious, the admirers of Gandhi's killer have found a new voice through social media. They have "come out". Their outpouring is linked to the Hindu-Muslim issue that features in the mainstream TV channels and in the FIRs filed at the police stations in violence-hit towns and villages.

Gandhi is hated by many and because of the rise of communalism, they have been emboldened to declare it in public. Godse's admirers, armed to "protect Hindus", roam around freely. One saffron-clad woman enacts the Gandhi murder scene with a toy pistol and fake blood. Her video goes viral. They display such bravery to be rewarded with the BJP ticket to fight the elections. A folk singer was interrupted and stopped from singing Gandhi's favourite song "Ishwar Allah Tero Naam" at a public function in Patna. And after the event she received threats.

To mark this birth anniversary, historian Vinay Lal had to write on "the killers of Gandhi in modern India". The newly introduced "muscular" politics is on his mind as he refers to Gandhi's killer, Nathuram Godse, angered by the Mahatma for effeminising Indian politics: "The so-called toxic masculinity that is on witness in the streets of every town and city in India is not only a manifestation of Hindu rage and a will to shape a decisive understanding of the past, but also a reaction to the androgynous values that Gandhi embodied and which the Hindu nationalist tacitly knows are enshrined in Indian culture. "What is different about the killers of Gandhi today is that they act with total impunity. They are aware of the fact that the present political dispensation is favourable to them, and that much of the 'ruling class' despises Gandhi. The official pieties surrounding Gandhi Jayanti may be nauseating to behold, but October 2 is a necessary provocation."

Prof. Vinay Lal says the display of respect is just to cover up the complete contempt and hatred for the "Mahatma". He refers to a poem circulating on WhatsApp calling Gandhi a fool and traitor to the nation and to the fact that Gandhi's assassin can be installed as a deity in a temple! Lal promises to write about this poem.

Prof. Avijit Pathak, who teaches sociology at the famous Jawaharlal Nehru University, writes: "Every year on October 2, I feel somewhat uneasy. From Rajghat (Gandhi Memorial) to Parliament, from the declaration of "pro-people" policies to the empty slogan initiated by the political class, I experience the death of Gandhi." He refers to the normalisation of the brute practice of stigmatising the "other" through lynching and cow-vigilantism. "From Gandhi's time of colonialism, religious reform and the nationalist movement, we seemed to have moved towards a new reality characterised by what I would regard as a mix of neoliberal capitalism and militant cultural nationalism, and market driven consumerism and technocratic develop-mentalism."

India's public broadcaster dutifully screened Richard Attenborough's famous film *Gandhi*. It shows the Mahatma stopping communal violence in Calcutta by going there and fasting. It shows Gandhi failing to prevent India's Partition on the basis of religion. The film moves the secular Hindus to tears with Gandhi calling Hindus and Muslims as the two eyes of Mother India. It angers the Hindu nationalists when Gandhi is shown pleading with Jinnah to give up his demand for Partition and to be the Prime Minister of an undivided India!

Those committed to social and economic equality feel enthused by Gandhi's advocacy of the untouchables and women. But the extremist patriarchs and the high-caste goons perhaps switch off the TV! The pacifists thank the film-maker for reminding the nation of Gandhi's warning that an eye for an eye will make the whole world blind. Some others see it as a conspiracy to weaken Hindus. Fortunately, the screening of the Attenborough film passed off peacefully! He made the film just in time. He shot it in India when ultra-nationalism was not in vogue. Political marginalisation of Muslims was unheard of. A civilisational state was yet to aspire to be a nation-state.

Attenborough's film introduces Gandhi's key principles even to those who only know that Gandhi was born on October 2 because on this day the schools and offices are closed. Through simple dialogue, the film highlights the foolishness of India imitating the Western consumption model, and not building self-reliant village communities, ignoring the value of handicrafts and local resources and indigenous skills. Gandhi's critics have considered these views quaint, anti-modernity and anti-industrialisation, while even some scientists admired Gandhi as an "innovator". R. A. Mashelkar coined the term "Gandhian engineering" to popularise his concept of frugal techniques for "doing more for less for more".

Ironically, it was Gandhi's call for *Swadeshi* (spirit of self-reliance) that fired the Indian scientists to develop high technology when India was denied it in fields ranging from super-computers to atomic energy and from space to military hardware. While roads in India named after Gandhi have shopping malls stuffed with imported underwear and toys, the leaders of America and Europe have become firm believers in *Swadeshi* by campaigning against imported goods and people!

But now, since some Western economists and activists have started admiring the Gandhian vision of sustainable development, the TV debates are not dominated by the sceptic experts. It was Gandhi who relentlessly tried to impress on the world leaders that the earth has enough for human needs but not for human greed!

Gandhi would have been quite amused to observe all this. One wishes to hear his typical humorous comments. He would have quipped on seeing a photo of his statue being vandalised or on reading a news report that the tallest statue in India will not be of the Father of the Nation but of his follower Sardar Patel!

Gandhi's birth anniversary yields a rich harvest of cartoons exposing the political elite's hypocrisy and its use of the ceremonies held on this national holiday. The expected editorials appear on the lip-service being paid to the Gandhian principles. The visual media displays the images and symbols associated with Gandhi. Gandhi remains relevant for publishers and for collectors of images and sketches. He remains invaluable for the brand mangers hired by politicians seeking votes and the commercial organisations seeking customers.

With his global appeal, Gandhi enhanced India's brand image. Gandhi even figured on an Apple hoarding in Silicon Valley! On this 149th birth anniversary, the government took a rare public diplomacy initiative by producing a video with collected clips of artists from 124 countries singing a line of Gandhi's favourite song that says that only the one who feels the pain of others can be said to be a good person. "*Vaishnava jan to tene kahiye, je peed parayi jaane hai...*", the 15th century devotional song in Gujarati, was in the set of hymns sung every day in Gandhi's Ashram. It was Prime Minister Narendra Modi's idea to present this song to a global audience.

A unique product popularised by Gandhi during the freedom struggle has got noticed internationally, thanks to some well-known fashion houses in France and other countries. Khadi, hand-woven cloth made from hand-spun yarn, attracted experts by the feel and look of its texture. For the same reason and not for the underlying Gandhian principle, many affluent Indians too started buying superfine khadi. On Gandhi's birth anniversary when khadi is subsidised by the government, New Delhi's flagship khadi store did a record sale exceeding 100,000 pounds sterling. It had to extend its business hours to handle increased footfall. So, in this case the ideological past profitably fused with the materialistic present.

Gandhi used his spinning wheel every day for meeting his own requirement. He spun yarn for a piece of lace that he gave as a wedding gift to Queen Elizabeth. (The Queen gave this piece of lace to Prime Minister Modi whose Minister promptly claimed that the gesture showed the esteem in which Modi is held! The Queen's magnanimity silenced those who want Britain to return the Kohinoor.)

Gandhi popularised khadi as a substitute for the British cloth. He propagated khadi as an instrument of uplifting the rural poor and making communities self-reliant. Khadi provided livelihood to countless village artisans. In the post-liberalisation India, the khadi movement suffered, and the impressive turnover of a few glamorous metropolitan outlets does not tell the entire story. Many khadi centres remain in a bad shape and heavily dependent on the state subsidy. Take just one example of a khadi centre opened by Gandhi in 1925 which is "dying, much like his legacy". The news report says the trust running the first-ever All India Spinners Association in a Punjab village was once famous for its khadi but is now dying of neglect. Today 20 of the State's 28 khadi trusts are running into losses. As a result, the artisans have either migrated or changed their profession. The famous fashion houses have given a "modern" touch to khadi. This year the simple but elegant Gandhi memorial in the national Capital has been equipped with digital displays! The memorial was spruced up after a court criticised its poor maintenance.

Displaying devotion to the museumised Father of the Nation and ignoring his principles have gone hand in hand for years. "Gandhi and iconography" has been studied by scholars. The image of his reading glasses came in handy for publicising a public sanitation campaign launched by Prime Minister Modi. All see the spectacles Gandhi used to wear and read the reports of sanitation workers killed by lethal gas while cleaning the sewage lines. The contractors do not give them the gas masks and the same tragedy is repeated over and over.

Incidents of the Dalits and Muslims being lynched are not rare. Gandhi would have launched a movement against the atrocities being committed against them. He would not have remained silent about the criminalisation of politics. Some 30 per cent of the legislators have criminal cases registered against them. The Supreme Court says it cannot bar them from fighting elections unless they are proven guilty.

India's youth today does not feel inspired by Gandhi who faces worse than neglect from the Hindu nationalists, capitalists, and the middle classes of the new India. The trusteeship principle has been abandoned by the capitalists many of whom had once responded to Gandhi's call. Moderation has been marginalised. The money-mad Indians indulging in conspicuous consumption wear their contempt for Gandhi on their sleeves. Sustainable development has never been taken seriously by the governments.

Do many new Indians read Albert Einstein's words that generations to come will scarcely believe that such a one as this ever in flesh and blood walked upon the earth? Or Nelson Mandela's words that Gandhi was the first person to show us the method of organised, disciplined, mass protest. Mahatma's grandson, Gopal Gandhi asks: What does one say of the 'mass' politics and the 'causes' of today's India? "On its thoroughfares, streets, by-lanes, village tracks and a hundred different hideouts, it damages, disfigures, destroys." Attenborough's film shows Gandhi's fast in Calcutta that ends communal violence and restores sanity. Viceroy Lord Mountbatten writes to Gandhi: "In the Punjab we have 55,000 soldiers and large-scale rioting on our hands, In Bengal our forces consist of one man, and there is no rioting. As a serving officer, as well as administration, may I be allowed to pay my tribute to the One-Man Boundary Force...?" Gandhi's fast made the evisceration of secularism a bit more difficult and kept the communal forces under check. It is said that Gandhi could work his magic on Britain, but he would have found it difficult to deal with Hitler's Germany. "One of Gandhi's achievements was to show Britons the reality of their own consciences, to reveal to them the gulf between their religious pretensions and political ideals, and their actual practice as imperialists," writes author George Woodcock.

Gandhi's Magic

Gandhi worked his magic on Indians of his time. Years later in mid-seventies, some Indians told V. S. Naipaul that since the death of Gandhi, truth has fled from India and the world! Naipaul saw an inversion of Gandhianism in the emergence of a violent Hindu cult like the Anand Marg and wrote about the "ease with which Hinduism can decline into barbarism". Now in

2018 there is no Anand Marg, but many Indians share Naipaul's fear. The 149th birth anniversary provokes one to fantasise about Gandhi's appearance in today's India. Suppose in his prayer meeting he talks about the Gita and the Sermon on the Mount in the same breath and says that the latter "went straight to my heart". Suppose he eulogises India's syncretic tradition and calls for freedom from fear and from cultural insecurity that have been inflicted on the people. Suppose he repeats his words that "religion is outraged when outrage is perpetrated in its name" and that "truth is God". Suppose he asks politicians not to tell lies. Suppose he tells them to stop abusing their opponents and start loving them. If that happens, Gandhi will have to abruptly end his prayer meeting and go on a fast! Will Indians ever again march on the street singing Gandhi's favourite song about the Supreme Being named Ishwar as well as Allah and praying to Him to bestow sanity on all human beings? Writing on Gandhi in an India stricken by sectarian violence, faux patriotism and jingoism causes gloom. A poem in Indian English written in the seventies by Nissim Ezekiel provides an antidote. *The Patriot* begins:

> *I am standing for peace and nonviolence.*
> *Why world is fighting and fighting*
> *Why all people of world*
> *Are not following Mahatma Gandhi,*
> *I am simply not understanding....*

A Hindu Pakistan

The perfidious Britain partitioned India and since then the divided family has been constantly at war. Pakistan kept attacking India militarily. India refrained from that but unleashed a war of ideas. The world recognised that India is not Pakistan which kept suffering setbacks in this invisible battlefield. Most Pakistanis favoured the Islamic national identity though some wanted their nation to be secular and democratic like India. Military dictator Gen. Zia wanted to counter India by unsheathing the weapon of Islam. He pushed Pakistan closer to the Arabic Islamic kingdoms, distancing it more from its inclusive Indian heritage and composite culture.

The rise of Islamic fundamentalism in a declared theocratic state increased the gulf between the two countries. However, the Indian political situation took a dramatic turn after the 2014 elections. In politics, things are never what they seem. So, the new ruling party that came to power attacking Pakistan in election speeches turned out to be one that abandoned the war of ideas, raising a white flag in that battlefield. In this limited context, paradoxically, India now looks like Pakistan's closet ally. Inching forward towards becoming a semi-theocratic state, India is set to vindicate the Pakistan model.

In Pakistan, the Islamic fundamentalists with influence over some terror groups are players on the political pitch. The new Indian Government gave a "befitting reply" by encouraging fiery Hindu leaders. In this case, poison only increased poison! Some saw in it a hidden hand of friendship designed for mutual political benefits. The rival communal groups that clash in public depend on each other for their very survival. The TV channels are most pleased since to remain profitable, they bank entirely on the entertainment value of the human versions of cockfights.

In 2014, a measure of convergence between the Pakistani and the new Indian model began to emerge. Poets get the intimations of a coming change. A Pakistani poetess saw the rise of Hindutva in the context of the suffering caused to Pakistan by Islamic fundamentalism. Fahmida Riaz recited in India her famous poem beginning: You turned out to be just like us. *Tum bilkul hum jaise nikle...*

Ironically, while the Pakistani poetess lamented, her liberal Indian audiences at that stage seemed unmindful of the serious consequences of what she foresaw. Dark clouds had started gathering then, but the liberals were simply delighted by her rhyme and reason! Literary dissidence, celebrated in small circles, hardly threatens even the Indian establishment.

Since the last parliamentary elections, India continues its path-breaking journey, politically marginalising a minority and letting small mobs do what those bound by law cannot do. The leader does not feel threatened by seminars on India's pluralistic traditions and multi-layered identity. In fact, his minions track the sleeping habits of every dissident academic.

With all this going on in India, Pakistan elects as its new Prime Minister, a former westernised playboy and much-married man, who had brought glory to Pakistan on the cricket field. He emerges as the new messiah – with a little help from the army, Islamic fundamentalists, and terrorist groups. He had practiced for his new role, assuming a religious persona and discarding his western dress with an indigenous sartorial make-up.

The inauguration of Pakistan's new Prime Minister is planned as a major event by the Garib Nawaz Foundation headed by a former intelligence officer who played a big role in the elections. The Pakistani foundation contacts its counterpart in India recalling that a Pakistani Prime Minister had gone to India for a similar event. It says it was the Indian Prime Minister's turn to join the show in Pakistan!

The Mahabharat Foundation promptly conveys the Indian Prime Minister's conditional acceptance of the invitation provided he is seated closest to the TV cameras. The letter marked secret says that the inauguration must be followed by a mass yoga session in Lahore conducted by Baba Ramdev so that Indian

TV anchors praise the Prime Minister for popularising Hindutva even in Pakistan! Another condition laid down by the Mahabharat Foundation is that the Pakistani Prime Minister should make friendly references to India in his inaugural speech. That will justify the trip. However, this honeymoon has to be switched off p at the beginning of 2019 when the Pakistan Prime Minister must start threatening India. In that phase, his Indian counterpart will start shooting down the Pakistani bricks with stones! The dust will fill the airwaves every night during India's poll campaign. "Please do not mind the Indian Prime Minister's anti-Pakistan tirade at the beginning of next year. We assure you that it would last no more than four months." Pakistan on its part must then stop lobbing bricks after the Indian elections to let New Delhi announce a breakthrough in the Indo-Pak relations! We will alert you about the start-stop operations through our secure parallel diplomacy communication channel.

The Mahabharat Foundation points out that Pakistan's victorious new leader benefitted politically from the outbreak of sectarian violence in India as it energised one of his constituencies. "Your incoming Prime Minister was helped by India being called 'Hindu Pakistan'. The Indian leader expects reciprocal benefits. Our mimicking you has served your interest. The transformed India has freed you from your isolation. Now no western activist will blame you alone in South Asia. Hindutva has helped you.

Imitation is the best form of admiration! So please stop looking at India as your enemy. See it as an ally. Thank us for letting you win the battle of ideas." The Indian foundation hopes that this mutually advantageous bargain will continue!

The poem by Fahmida Riaz translated from Urdu by Shabana Mir:

You were just like us!

So, it turned out you were just like us!
Where were you hiding all this time, buddy?
That stupidity, that ignorance
we wallowed in for a century –
look, it arrived at your shores too!
Many congratulations to you!

Raising the flag of religion,
I guess now you'll be setting up Hindu Raj?
You too will commence to muddle everything
You, too, will ravage your beautiful garden.

You, too, will sit and ponder –
I can tell preparations are afoot –
who is [truly] Hindu, who is not.
I guess you'll be passing fatwas soon!

Here, too, it will become hard to survive.
Here, too, you will sweat and bleed.
You'll barely make do joylessly.
You will gasp for air like us.

I used to wonder with such deep sorrow.
And now, I laugh at the idea:
it turned out you were just like us!
We weren't two nations after all!
To hell with education and learning.
Let's sing the praises of ignorance.
Don't look at the potholes in your path:
bring back instead the times of yore!

Practice harder till you master
the skill of always walking backwards.
Let not a single thought of the present
break your focus upon the past!
Repeat the same thing over and over –
over and over, say only this:
How glorious was India in the past!
How sublime was India in days gone by!

Then, dear friends, you will arrive
and get to heaven after all.
Yep. We've been there for a while now.
Once you are there,
once you're in the same hellhole,
keep in touch and tell us how it goes!

The original:

तुम बिल्कुल हम जैसे निकले

तुम बिल्कुल हम जैसे निकले

अब तक कहां छिपे थे भाई

वो मूरखता, वो घामड़पन

जिसमें हमने सदी गंवाई
आखिर पहुँची द्वार तुम्हारे
अरे बधाई, बहुत बधाई।
प्रेत धर्म का नाच रहा है
कायम हिंदू राज करोगे ?
सारे उल्टे काज करोगे !
अपना चमन ताराज़ करोगे !
तुम भी बैठे करोगे सोचा
पूरी है वैसी तैयारी
कौन है हिंदू, कौन नहीं है
तुम भी करोगे फ़तवे जारी
होगा कठिन वहाँ भी जीना
दाँतों आ जाएगा पसीना
जैसी तैसी कटा करेगी
वहाँ भी सब की साँस घुटेगी
माथे पर सिंदूर की रेखा
कुछ भी नहीं पड़ोस से सीखा!

क्या हमने दुर्दशा बनाई
कुछ भी तुमको नजर न आयी?
कल दुख से सोचा करती थी
सोच के बहुत हँसी आज आयी
तुम बिल्कुल हम जैसे निकले
हम दो कौम नहीं थे भाई।
मश्क करो तुम, आ जाएगा
उल्टे पाँव चलते जाना

ध्यान न मन में दूजा आए
 बस पीछे ही नजर जमाना
भाड़ में जाए शिक्षा-विक्षा
अब जाहिलपन के गुन गाना।

आगे गड्ढा है यह मत देखो
लाओ वापस, गया ज़माना
एक जाप सा करते जाओ
बारम्बार यही दोहराओ
कैसा वीर महान था भारत
कैसा आलीशान था-भारत
फिर तुम लोग पहुँच जाओगे
बस परलोक पहुँच जाओगे
हम तो हैं पहले से वहाँ पर
तुम भी समय निकालते रहना
अब जिस नरक में जाओ वहाँ से
चिट्ठी-विट्ठी डालते रहना।

--- फ़हमीदा रियाज़

I too am in the same boat

Allegations of being pro-Pakistani comes in handy for winning elections. One election victory resulted from a campaign that focussed not on the state's problems but on a tirade against Mia Musharraf of Pakistan. Another election was won following a fake report that some Congress leaders had a secret meeting with Pakistanis. This writer tries to comfort an independent journalist targeted by the state and the trollers:

Dear Friend,

I hope your moving confessions about your association with Pakistani men and women have not moved the beat constable into action. Perhaps you are lucky that we do not have a nationalistic police chief. Do you still have access to the internet and you are at home? I hope this email from your well-wisher is not lost because your hate-mail-filled box can take no more.

I am sorry you have let me and other friends down by recalling these damning details about our Pakistan visit. It implicates me because of our past association. You should not have referred to the Pakistan visit. A babu is scrutinising the list of the correspondents who accompanied Rajiv Gandhi to Islamabad. Trollers will be tipped off and asked to demand action. Some may raise slogans against Rajiv Gandhi's visit to Pakistan.

You know what is being done to Nehru in social media.

Some of us face a bigger trouble. You did not return from Lahore with beautifully embroidered woollen shawls and onyx table-lamps but between you and me, I did. I would be forced to disclose that the Pakistani shopkeepers at first refused to accept any payment but when I insisted, they gave a huge discount with immense goodwill for guests from India! At that time they never imagined that India would ever want to stop their water supply. If we start confessing like you, those poor shopkeepers of Lahore will face a double whammy. They will be harassed both by the Pakistani agencies and Indian agents. They will face two different charges: Helping Indians and bribing Indians.

I was hesitant to tell you about the shopkeepers of Lahore because these days retired vegetarian diplomats make nasty comments about Indians going to Pakistan for the love of *biryani!* Belonging to the "befitting reply brigade", they are now wiser and disown their ministry's earlier non-confrontationist Pakistan policy. They are for muscular foreign policy. They target even a virile Punjabi who as the Prime Minister invoked *panjabiyat* to win Pakistan's friendship! Let me say in my defence that i am not a Punjabi and I have no fond memories of Anarkali!

Did you have to confess when accusing is the favourite past-time of our leaders? Do you not realise that when a mob overturns a car, a poet has to run for safety?

I am a bit anxious these days because I do not wear a T-shirt with the slogan: I Love India. I do not keep at home the tri-colour, made of *khadi* or Chinese silk, to wave when asked to do so.

Unlike you, I lack courage to present myself at a local police station. My hand and heart will tremble if the sub-inspector asks me to scribble three words in triplicate "I Love India" or "Jai Shri Ram". I still want to live in a culture in which "I Love You" is never said by a truly loving spouse. A heroine declares that if one is compelled to say these three words, love loses meaning! And you know what all goes on in the culture in which this statement is made mindlessly a dozen times a day.

The local beat constable frightens me. He is more powerful than Pakistan's President. As you know, our senior editors writing fiery editorials against the dictator of Pakistan hesitate to print a letter to editor against the local police inspector.

These days a few ruffians humble the mighty film industry and the heroes who kill dozens of villains in three hours! Our strongest Rambo-hero kept mum when a noted Muslim actor was asked for no reason to go to Pakistan. A big name of Bollywood looked like a hostage declaring love for his country in front of a camera held by a gunman.

I have digressed. I just want to ask you why did you make such confessions and get identified by the non-state actors doing the state's job? Such actors have proliferated because of India's transformation. Here as in the US, the administration outsources any illegal task to private agencies. So the person coming after me will have no police uniform! You may call me a wimp but like many of my countrymen, I have learnt that at a time of the great transformation of this great nation, discretion is better part of valour. But you slipped.

The one who recovered the incriminating items from the JNU dustbins and shared the total figure with the nationalistic TV channels, will disclose all details about you. The channels will broadcast that ninety lakh, eighty thousand and seven hundred seven Pakistanis read your confessions and six million more watched you on the TV. These figures will rule the airwaves for the next three days. Your popularity in Pakistan will be the firm evidence of your being a traitor.

Why did you out yourself during this crazy time? Were you moved by poet Dinkar who wrote that not to take a stand would be counted as a crime by history? Was it because your conscience pricked and you could stand cowardice no more? Or were you afraid that soon all this will be discovered by the Organisation for Discovering Un-Indian Activity? Or were you tipped off by a liberal bureaucrat that those who confess before October 30 will face no action under a voluntary disclosure scheme? That means the anti-national Indians tracked by the *Desh Droh Samapti Sena* after October 30 will face much harsher punishment. Please tell us if such a voluntary disclosure scheme is coming because then millions of Indians can start confessing in order to save their bodies and souls.

And one last request: If you are still at home, please do not switch on any of the nationalistic TV channels tonight unless you are still in a mood to inflict self-harm. And if you are not at home, I hope unlike the notorious dons, you have no access to TV in your car. I will be greatly relieved if you tell me that you are at home. And will be delighted if you tell me that behind the closed doors, you are listening to a Pakistani singer or the India-loving Pakistani poet who lamented: "You have turned out to be like us!"

Wishing you safety,

Your Friend and Fellow Traveller

Delhi RWA Sounds the Bugle!

The Jangpura Extension Residents Welfare Association asked the Congress leader Mani Shankar Aiyar and his non-resident daughter to move out of the colony for hurting the religious sentiments of the Hindus. (Ms. Suranya Aiyar had provoked the RWA by going on a fast for communal harmony and expressing her views on Ayodhya's new Ram Temple.) The RWA President was hugely applauded by the Modi-devotees! The IT Cell came out in his support. Many residents informed him of their neighbours' illegal activities. He got hundreds of bouquets and one brickbat. Here is a random selection of their unwritten social media posts:

Congratulations for issuing the notice to the Congress leader! You went where ED and CBI have not gone. Your commitment to Hindutva has been noted by the top leadership and the party would invite you to fight the parliamentary elections.

You have set an example for other RWAs. As a poll strategist, I am factoring in the role of RWAs in my presentation to the Prime Minister. I am sure he would call upon the RWAs to do their sacred duty. Every RWA President will be made Panna Pramukh for the elections. The Government will give the top civilian award to the RWA President who collects the highest number of residents behind the Hindutva flag.

We in this colony cannot tolerate the *sickular* residents. We thank you for warning the anti-Hindutva elements out to abuse Hindu beliefs. Now no one would dare to defile a sacred Hindu ceremony.

I am broadcasting your message to millions of my subscribers to ensure that Mani Shankar Aiyar pays for his daughter's sin and does not get a house in any city. We live in Jangpura and are ready to fight a jang against sickular residents.

I am inspired to move to Jangpura following your bold stand. I see an opportunity in the coming distress sale of his house by Mani Shankar Aiyar. Please keep me informed.

One member, who fought the association election against you, sends messages admiring Nehru and Gandhi. You will face this sickular man again when you seek re-election. Clip his wings now.

Please launch an inquiry into the conduct of the RWA past president who allowed the entry of Mani Shankar Aiyar into this colony. We should make the conditions for admission stricter.

I want to fast on next Tuesday. It is for worshipping Lord Hanuman, not for communal harmony. I need the RWA's permission in writing to avoid any controversy later.

The loud noise of Pop music coming from my neighbour's house disturbed me last night. Would you please ask House No. 654 to play Ram Bhajans instead?

My wife has started watching dirty pictures. If the RWA issues a notice in this regard, she may stop this activity.

My neighbour invited me for a *havan* conducted by an Arya Samaj Pandit. The Pandit gave a *pravachan*. His tirade against idol-worship, coming in the wake of the consecration of the grand Ram Temple, shocked us. The Association should stop such activity as it hurts our religious sentiments.

I am letting out my house for which the highest offer has come from a low-caste single woman. I hope you will clear the tenancy. Some associations have a problem with single women. Please share with me the RWA blacklist of castes and religions.

You warned one resident against spreading secular propaganda in our WhatsApp Group. He stopped posting subversive material. Now, the resident of House No. 592 has started the same mischief. RWA must stop him.

I am glad to note that most of our residents are pucca deshbhakt. They forward the posts on the Hindutva plan of action and our beloved Prime Minister's latest photo. One TV fellow calls them WhatsApp Uncles to malign them.

The radio in our community club is not working. This Sunday, we missed the *Man ki Baat* programme. Please install a new set before next Sunday.

After your recent public warning, some of us held a secret meeting and decided to regularly report to you every undesirable activity in the colony. Last night, a police constable visited my neighbour on the right. Some fishy things are going on. Please investigate.

I spotted a communist leaders and a Chinese-looking man coming out of my neighbour's house at 11.30 last night. Earlier, I heard these people making subversive speeches.

I appreciate your constant vigilance. I saw a mini-skirt-clad woman coming out of the House No. 420 last night. My religious sensibility was deeply hurt. Also, my female neighbour has started coming home past midnight. Please keep an eye and act.

All kinds of people have started buying houses in this colony. RWA must get to know their antecedents. They should be asked to fill a questionnaire about their religious and political beliefs. I am glad you demanded the Aadhar Card in one case. Please insist on the marriage certificate and copy it to all original members. Our Prime Minister suggested that the password for the mobile phone should be shared by every member of the family. This way we can keep an eye on the younger generation. It should be made compulsory in the colony.

In House No. 491 lives a JNU professor. He is trying to brainwash youngsters. His university produces anti-national students.

You must inculcate the Hindutva spirit among the residents by levying the Ram Temple Tax. If any resident defaults, he should leave the colony.

Your call for having Jai Shri Ram chanting session every Tuesday got an excellent response. RWA must organise a free visit to Ayodhya. There is a Government scheme for such trips. Please apply.

A *Sunder Kand Path* will be held at my house on Sunday. Hope RWA will organise the *prasad* for the participants. We have set a record of holding such paths so this colony is eligible for a Government grant for establishing a temple in the compound.

A non-vegetarian dhaba has come up adjoining our colony. RWA must get it closed.

A new bangle shop has been started in our market by a non-Hindu. I fear for our women in the wake of news reports of Love Jihad. Please get this shop closed.

One brave resident dissents

I was shocked to read your notice asking a family to move out because of the protest fast by someone who does not even live in our colony. Some RWAs have become an instrument of the communal forces instead of looking after the welfare of the members. Do not be encouraged by the current toxic atmosphere and the ruling establishment. You defamed one of our members who happens to be a Congress leader. You have no legal authority to issue such a *firman*. Please cease and desist before someone files a case against you. You know me as a *sickular* person but never dare to call me by such names.

The RWA President stays silent.

Donation of Cows

The Indian Prime Minister's gift of cows to Rwanda set Twitterdom on fire because the liberals know nothing about the Hindu dharma. Godaan yields a boon – a political victory in this life and *Moksha* in after-life. The holy ritual helps in absolving one of sin and getting divine blessings. Many posts urged Modi to send a *Gau Rakshak Dal* (Cow Protection Brigade) to Rwanda -- a country of beefeaters.

Fiction antedates events. In a book published long before Narendra Modi's Rwanda visit, a fictional Indian Prime Minister gifts cows to Great Britain during his visit there. Two diplomats in the Indian High Commission in London discuss the gift their Prime Minister is bringing with him. An excerpt from this writer's book *The Twain*:

GODAAN

Indian High Commission, London

RAMU MANDAL: We strayed from our main topic.
JAM MATHUR: Into an airplane loo!
RAMU MANDAL: Let's return to the PM's visit. I am sure Lalluvaji will get good publicity here.
JAM MATHUR: How? Without knowing English?
RAMU MANDAL: He will make himself heard loud

and clear in Hindi! He is an emerging world statesman!

JAM MATHUR: Brits have statesmen, we have tyrants!

RAMU MANDAL: The High Commissioner should invite the editors for a curry lunch.

JAM MATHUR: That will not help. A British journalist cannot be bribed. The only way your Lalluva can land on the front pages is if he slips and fall. One Indian leader managed it that way.

RAMU MANDAL: You want the Prime Minister of India to be a laughingstock!

JAM MATHUR: If he walks on the Thames, he will grab headlines.

RAMU MANDAL: Lalluvaji does have yogic powers.

JAM MATHUR: A Sinking Indian, like the Flying Dutchman, will amuse Britons!

RAMU MANDAL: You overlook Lalluvaji's unique selling point, his rustic appearance.

JAM MATHUR: They will laugh at him.

RAMU MANDAL: They would love him. Lalluvaji does not provoke envy. Lalluvaji makes them feel superior! His visage and apparel assure Them that we are not like Them. Nehru made them feel inferior.

JAM MATHUR: But they want us to be like Them.

RAMU MANDAL: Rhetoric! They say why you can't be like us. But if you take on Their habits and thoughts, you are told: "How dare you be like us?'

JAM MATHUR: You can never be like Them!

RAMU MANDAL: They don't really want you to be like Them! The Bengalee Baboo matched Their wits! He knew their language, literature, and history better than many educated Englishmen, not just the white barrack room boys and railway yard lads.

JAM MATHUR: Bengalee Baboo invited contempt.

RAMU MANDAL: The English categorise human beings. They love the underdog.

JAM MATHUR: The hangdog look is nothing to brag about.

RAMU MANDAL: The British media would love Lalluvaji cuddling a calf.

JAM MATHUR: Why can't he kiss babies?

RAMU MANDAL: The Brits like animals, not children

JAM MATHUR: What do we serve at the Reception for the Prime Minister?

RAMU MANDAL: No champagne. A Pure Milk Reception it will be. Exotic!

JAM MATHUR: What! A diplomatic Reception without wines?

RAMU MANDAL: Lalluvaji's lineage is traced to Lord Krishna and milkmaids. The glasses will have the stamp: "Milked in India - Not of Mad Cows."

JAM MATHUR: It will send a wrong signal to the Scotch industry which has big plans in India. It wants the PM to inaugurate a new distillery in Scotland.

RAMU MANDAL: Britain wants more market access and a free flow of Scotch in India. It asked India to "cut the exorbitant tariff which makes the bottles from here too expensive for the average Indian drinker".

JAM MATHUR: And our response is to hold a milk reception!

RAMU MANDAL: Let's not think of trade all the time. The first-ever Milk Reception will promote Indian culture.

JAM MATHUR: Milk and India have already acquired a funny association. When Hindu Gods drank milk in London temples, our Press Counsellor got into a soup. British TV crews went on a rampage in temples and he couldn't explain Lord Ganesha's drinking habit.

RAMU MANDAL: It was alien to the tradition of blood and wine!

JAM MATHUR: The milk reception will revive the miracle story.

RAMU MANDAL: Don't doubt miracles. In Patna, a statue of Lord Shiva shook his trident. It was taken to be a warning of a nuclear firestorm!

JAM MATHUR: Indian journalists, if denied whisky, will not be amused. The British will snigger. We will displease both sides.

RAMU MANDAL: Whether we offer milk or whisky, the British Press will write on the rodent on an Air India plane.

JAM MATHUR: We do nothing to change their perception. Nothing! Do we supply them the TV footage of our space research?

RAMU MANDAL: Unlike China, India did not get a Needham to project its scientific competence. British intellectuals promoted imperialism. J. Brownskie took *The Ascent of Man* to be the ascent of the Western Man. To Kenneth Clark, Civilisation meant the Western Civilisation.

JAM MATHUR: What gift is our Prime Minister bringing for his hosts?

RAMU MANDAL: He came to know that British cows have gone mad.

JAM MATHUR: So?

RAMU MANDAL: He is bringing 11 sane Indian cows. It will be an act of Godaan. Of course, you know nothing about the significance of donating cows. Heard of the great Hindi writer Munshi Premchand?

JAM MATHUR: Good God! An Indian bearing such a gift will be a laughingstock!

RAMU MANDAL: Why? Indira Gandhi was gifted a horse in Austria. She didn't look into its mouth. Is the horse superior to cow?

JAM MATHUR: Austrians giving a horse is different. An Indian leader arriving in England with a herd of cows! Preposterous!

RAMU MANDAL: Why?

JAM MATHUR: John Stuart Mill called India "England's cattle farm". This gift will reinforce that image.

RAMU MANDAL: The Brits knew India as a milch cow. They will welcome the cows alighting from AI Gajraj, with a cleaner in tow.

JAM MATHUR: Apart from shit and milk, the cow yields political capital in India!

RAMU MANDAL: That is why our Prime Minister chose cows as India's gift. His political stock will go up when Indian TV channels show cows alighting in London amid fanfare.

JAM MATHUR: Some Hindu Manch M.P.s, will use that gesture to defect to the Prime Minister's party
RAMU MANDAL: Lalluvaji will break his predecessor's vote bank once Indian cows are ceremonially welcomed in London and that image of telecast in India.
JAM MATHUR: The cow is no laughing matter. Cow-worshippers kill men in the name of cows. Anything is possible in the Republic of Unreason!
RAMU MANDAL: When India was being turned into Abusurdistan, you didn't dare to utter a word! With Lalluvaji in power, you exercise freedom of speech. Lalluvaji has the ability to win the minds and hearts of Britons! We should use him.
JAM MATHUR: Our public diplomacy events will cost a huge sum.
RAMU MANDAL: For the PM's visit, money is no constraint. To mark the PM's visit, we must organise an exhibition on the life of Mahatma Gandhi.
JAM MATHUR: Who is interested in the Father of the Nation, murdered by an Indian who was proud of committing fratricide! Britons would enjoy a show by a sexy celebrity from Mumbai! Tallyho Tobacco Plc would sponsor a tour by the Goa Gay Band Baza. A statue of Kipling could be erected in the foyer of the Nehru Centre. In America, Kipling is classified as an Indian poet because he was born in Bombay. The first Indo-Anglian poet to enter the history of English literature! Kipling is Britain's most favourite poet!
RAMU MANDAL: Let's get back to the PM's visit.

Lalluvaji will create a buzz about India!

JAM MATHUR: We need a human interest story to feed the media! A spectacle on an East-West theme. Re-enact the Indian Maharajas' encounters with English concubines in London! Indian Maharajkumaris and their lovers in London!

RAMU MANDAL: A comedy based on an English actress marrying an Indian. Or a tragedy based on an English daughter-in-law abusing the husband's parents.

JAM MATHUR: Why not hold an exhibition of the ivory pieces once owned by the Indian Maharajas? These are stored in the British Museum basement. Naked white women dancing before a brown Maharaja to the strains of western classical music. The people here will find these erotic. You will see these as an assertion of our power over Them.

RAMU MANDAL: I hope our Lalluvaji performs brilliantly.

JAM MATHUR: It is the performance of our ministers that lands us in trouble. Hope Lalluvaji is briefed how to behave in Britain. Every phoren-going Minister should undergo a compulsory course in manners.

RAMU MANDAL: How to behave with air hostesses and female escorts should be the first lesson.

JAM MATHUR: I hope we do not have to organise some special diet for your Lalluvaji. One Indian Prime Minister travelled to the Soviet Union with a charcoal *angheeti* and his cook. This PM may also bring his cook and pure provisions. Take your Lalluvaji to Savoy for a propah English supper.

RAMU MANDAL: Good God, the Savoy Bill will be debated in Parliament for days. The press will scream that the bill's amount would have fed an entire Indian village. "Parliament Rocked Again", will be the front-page headline as the opposition M.P.s will create unruly scenes.

JAM MATHUR: Parliament gets rocked anyway! Anyway, what do we project? Outdated socialism or resurgent Hinduism or consensual capitalism?

RAMU MANDAL: We check with the PMO. Better still, we check here with NRI Seth Bhatija who will host our dear Leader in private. He knows the PM's mind. He minds his purse. The PM's interaction with the NRIs will be fraught with danger.

JAM MATHUR: Any meeting with the Brit-Indians is always risky. The problem begins with the guest list and ends with faction fights in the presence of a visiting minister. The last *vin d'honneur* here led to a controversy in Indian Parliament. We will discuss the Brit-Indians after lunch.

Rising roar of faux faith
in poll-bound India

2019

If you hear the rising roar of faith, it is election-time in India. Belief in God is stronger than any political belief. Faith rushes to fill ideological vacuum and cleanses politics of residual ideological content. Religious fervour, injected into a poll campaign, boosts popular interest in elections, promotes identity politics and alters voting preferences. That is why the ruling BJP has made religious polarisation its electoral strategy. It consolidates Hindu votes by propagating Hindutva, a militant and less inclusive version of Hinduism.

The BJP leaders including L K Advani were called "Hindu fundamentalists". Knowing that the term "fundamentalism" has acquired bad odour in the context of Islam, Advani declared that they were "Hindu nationalists" not "Hindu fundamentalists". He was correct because going back to the fundamentals of his religion would mean the Vedic tradition which will rob the proposed Ram temple of all significance!

His 1992 movement to build a Ram temple generated a toxic mix of religion and nationalism and turned it into a potent political weapon. Till then the political armies marching under the saffron flag had not been able to make much headway. Advani's historic journey to Ayodhya in his belief-driven 'chariot' led to the demolition of a mosque and the killings of Muslims and Hindus.

Noted documentary maker Anand Patwardhan says TV serial Ramayan, watched by millions, paved the way for the demolition of the Babri mosque. "A bow-and-arrow bearing Ram entered every household and every heart." There was no social media then, but TV too promotes pop religion and causes social disharmony. Some partisan TV channels go all out to fuel religious polarisation.

During the past four years, the sectarian poison has spread much more, with incidents of mob rule becoming frequent. It has seeped into "cultured" upper-class Hindu homes. The kind of people involved in violence matters. Intent is important. While sectarian violence can break out in the best of times, mental pollution sustains the process of violence.

The BJP finds assemblies of Hindu monks in saffron politically valuable. Communal worship and public observance of rituals make good TV that spreads the message of Hindutva. Mythology-based TV drama helps. The Hindu nationalists willfully ignore the theological complexities of Vedic thought and their faith's glorious history of disputation and argumentation. They try to enforce a simplistic doctrine that supersedes the rich variegated strands of thought and belief. In order to collect Hindus on a single political platform, they want to create a central creed and designate one holy book. Above all, they want to establish the primacy of warrior-king Lord Ram. The people must feel, not think.

To get more Hindu votes, the party must fuel envy and animosity by blaming a secular government for "appeasing Muslims. In an election speech, Prime Minister Narendra Modi made a subtle reference to the Hindu cremation grounds and the Muslim graveyards. This was a hint that the socialist state government's provision of building walls around the graveyards to protect these from encroachment was discriminatory.

In the run-up to elections, vicious statements are made to cause tensions and promote orthodoxy. What the BJP spokesmen shout at times during TV discussions is unfit to print. The Muslim spokesmen shout back, which serves the purpose of all sectarian forces. The atmosphere reeks of bigotry and hostility towards the "other" faith. Some children hear their parents say that so and so should be elected since he would "fix" a minority. They learn that "when we say prayers loudly, it is worship, when they worship loudly, it is disturbing noise!" Children learn that "when we say prayers loudly, it is worship, when they worship loudly, it is disturbing noise!"

As the BJP gained power, the Hindutva got many new adherents. The "secular" leaders who used to condemn Narendra Modi's sectarianism, now see a messiah in him. Several Hindutva groups have sprung up under official patronage. Their activity highlights the anti-minority dimension of Hindutva. The divisive rhetoric flows with force as the police and some in the lower rungs of judiciary have turned partisan.

Some BJP leaders make weird statements that can be described as anti-science and irrational. The power of superstition has increased. A poll candidate declares that if she is elected, the police will not be allowed to check child marriage! The fashion of wearing religion on one's sleeves has caught on. Commercial interests promote more religious festivals. The outbreak of religiosity is to be seen to be believed. More Hindu pilgrims march for miles and miles to fetch the holy Ganga water. Charitable Hindus set up tents on the footpaths for feeding the tired pilgrims. This public spectacle disrupts traffic and at times results in clashes.

Meditation and quiet contemplation are not popular. The attendance in temples has gone up. More Hindu temples, as also mosques and churches, are being built as a result of growing prosperity. Competitive communalism has made mosques more crowded. The temple loudspeaker's volume is increased to match the sound coming from the neighbouring mosque. In this atmosphere of religious rivalry, private contemplation and meditation get devalued.

A brainchild of the Hindu nationalists, Hindutva is not eclectic and dialogic. It has been honed as a powerful tool for political mobilisation through incendiary divisive statements. Hindutva fiercely seeks converts. When popularised by a charismatic divisive leader, its political dimension overshadows spirituality.

In the current atmosphere of intolerance, the political message of Hindutva is amplified through social media by political activists including the Non-Resident Indians. Little is heard about the huge difference between Hindutva and Hinduism known over the centuries as Sanatan Dharma.

To understand the distortion of Hinduism, one has to be familiarised with the real thing. Hinduism, tolerant and inclusive, includes principles taken from different faiths and cultures. Even before its interaction with Islam and Christianity, Hinduism assimilated new ideas and practices while transiting from the Vedic to the Puranic period. Hinduism sanctifies sacrifices of the Vedic Aryans as well as the rituals of primitive tribes. Not all Hindu gods are Aryan gods. Hinduism has no central creed and no central authority, nor does it prescribe one specific book to follow. It is not based on a revelation granted to a prophet. Hindus do not consider themselves to be the "chosen people". They do not consider their faith to be superior to others. This democratic religion, presided over by a Parliament of Gods, has no founder. Hinduism has no central creed and no central authority, nor does it prescribe one specific book to follow... This democratic religion, presided over by a Parliament of Gods, has no founder.

The Divine can be reached through any of the several different ways. Two prominent ones are the path of knowledge and the path of devotion. This is a simple journalistic statement about a faith whose complexities even scholars find hard to fathom. Hinduism is studded with elegant metaphysical knots and strange paradoxes. It offers infinite choice. Those who do not like the idea of a galaxy of gods and goddesses can take comfort from the Rig Vedic thought that all the many gods are manifestation of the One Reality. Hindus revere a saint-poet who does not believe in rituals or external formalities and for whom God lives, not in a temple or a mosque but in his devotion.

A Hindu can choose from the nine specified ways to perform devotion or devise one of his own. Astounding diversity is reflected not just in innumerable gods and ways of worship but also in the multiple versions of its sacred books and philosophical treatises. Rituals vary from region to region and from caste to caste. There is choice in the ways of dying. Hindus are generally cremated, but thousands of Hindus are given earthen and riverine burials. The variety of thought content, rituals and devotional practices meet the needs of all sections of society, ranging from the intellectual elite to the illiterate masses.

Millions recite 1000 names of one God and 1000 names of a Goddess. A sacred text features Mahadevi, literally the Great Goddess who encompasses the thousands of local and regional devis as well as the pan-Indian goddesses. Each god or goddess is worshipped in several forms. Columnist Shobha Narayan writes about her mother being part of an ancient Hindu lineage linked to goddess worship called Sri Vidya. She says: "It is visually and aesthetically very beautiful – with flowers, incense, oil lamps, hand gestures called mudras, sacred drawings called mandalas or yantras, and the chanting of mantras. Mudra, mandala and mantra, the triumvirate as it were – is at the root of this goddess cult."

Hindus of one region may accord primacy to one form which may not be worshipped at all by those of another region. Then, the veneration of natural forces such as the monsoon rains and trees and of animals is common among those living in forests. Ideas and practices from the margins have been leaking into the mainstream.

This interplay is seen in Hindu religious art and objects made by Muslims. They participate in Hindu religious festivals. Eminent Muslim musicians played in Hindu temples. Muslim poets wrote devotional songs in praise of Hindu Gods. A most devout Brahmin, Congress leader Kamalapati Tripathi, had a Muslim assistant to clean and arrange the idols in his home temple before daily worship.

In the absence of a set form of worship, a Hindu is free to act according to his individual belief. What counts is not belief but conduct, as stated by philosopher S. Radhakrishnan, who was India's President. No wonder Hinduism embraces believers and non-believers, the theist and the atheist, the sceptic and the agonistic.

Scholar Kshiti Mohan Sen says the uniting force among the enormous variety of religious beliefs and ceremonies in Hinduism has been the belief in a basic code of behaviour. Today he would have seen more Hindus indulging in an un-Hindu-like conduct at the behest of political leaders. The examples include the lynching of alleged beef transporters, intimidating women temple-goers, disrupting a Christian prayer meeting and demolishing a mosque.

The influence of Hinduism over Islam and Christianity is reflected in the Sufi tradition and in Christian meditation and Christian Vedanta. It can be seen in the global Hare Krishna movement. Hinduism also contributed to the New Age faiths! Muslims and Christians extended the reach of the sacred Hindu literature by translating it and even helped preserve some of it. This is never recalled while the voters are constantly reminded of the Hindu temples destroyed by the Moghuls.

India's syncretic tradition can be attributed mainly to the diversity of Hinduism that has a history of several philosophical turns. Of course, this diversity leads to confusion over certain precepts. Differing practices and various interpretations of the same sacred text, in the absence of a validating central authority, result in mixed-up theological concepts and endless arguments. Thus theological dissent always got accommodated. Hinduism is suffused with paradoxes. The Divine is unimaginable and unknowable and yet the Divine is imagined in countless forms appearing in abstract and representational art and as idols of stone and metal. Hindus worship gods both in iconic and aniconic forms. The deity in thousands of rural temples is just a painted stone. Devotion takes the form of meditation, quiet contemplation, lighting sacrificial fire, loud out-of-tune community singing, disciplined congregational chanting, ritual bathing, fasting or even social service since God lives in every human being.

There is latent divinity in every being and everything. There is an external God and the God within. God is a distant entity but then the devotee is also part of Brahman, the universal soul! Aham Brahmāsmi in general terms implies the unity of individual self with the Absolute. Thus, divinity is shared by every human being. Divisive rhetoric has to be foreign to Hinduism which says: Thou art That (*Tat Tvam Asi*).

Scholars observe how Hinduism, when hijacked for political purposes, gets vulgarised. The devotees are encouraged to display faux religiosity. The Sarkari (pro-Government) "seers", in their so-called religious discourses, bless the Prime Minister. The ruling party needs their endorsement, the seers want political patronage. The seers are sought after by politicians more than by spiritual aspirants.

Respected heads of genuine spiritual institutions keep quiet about the misuse of religion for elections. Surely, they are pained by the distortion of their faith tradition, seeing an immense idea being reduced to a dismal creed. Islamic leaders get blamed for not condemning the misuse of their faith by politicians and terrorists. One may ask where have the Hindu spiritual leaders gone? Islamic leaders get blamed for not condemning the misuse of their faith by politicians and terrorists. One may ask where have the Hindu spiritual leaders gone? The distortion of Hinduism does not provoke much reaction while many Christian communities debate spirituality vs. institutionalised religion. There is no such discourse in Hinduism, notwithstanding its tradition of argumentation. It is left to a few secular politicians and the leftists to offer a trenchant criticism of Hindutva. They reason well but they cannot influence those swayed by the men in saffron robes. The leftists, not well-versed in India's spiritual traditions, have little leverage with the faithful. Only firm believers protesting against the "hijacking of our religion" can make an impact. They can increase the public understanding of Hinduism unsullied by politics.

Those rushing to demolish a mosque or build a temple on a disputed plot know nothing about a faith that assimilated various religions and cultural movements. They are familiar with folklore, mythology and miracles and black magic but unaware of the Vedic Song of Creation that wonders whether even the Creator knows all! That kind of questioning will be considered blasphemy and a punishable offence in some other religions. The sacred texts of Hinduism make bigotry unthinkable. In the wake of the Babri mosque's demolition, Prof. Amartya Sen attributed growing fanaticism to the neglect of the classics in education.

Fanaticism characterises politicisation of religion and that retards reforms. The Supreme Court lifted the ban on the entry of young women into a Hindu temple. The BJP launched an agitation against the entry of young women in order to uphold a "sacred tradition". However, the same ruling party was all for abolishing the traditional Muslim custom of instant divorce because it oppressed Muslim women. The BJP Government undertook the noble mission of reforming Islam but considers reformation of Hinduism as a no-go area. The BJP president advises law courts to refrain from hurting Hindu sentiments and to pass only such judgments that are "implementable"!

Every old faith tradition accumulates undesirable rituals and practices and Hinduism, being a product of many cultures and cults, is more prone to do so. In its long journey, Hinduism acquired and discarded many questionable rituals. It abolished some practices partly due to the influence of Christian values but mainly by recollecting its own glorious Vedic past. There was recognition of the corruptive influence of idolatry, child-marriage, self-immolation by widows and untouchability that had no place in its ancient culture. Commenting on this process of reforms and renewal, scholar Kshiti Mohan Sen writes that the impact of the West produced new schools of thought which emphasised old doctrines. Hinduism has a rich history of reforms. Swami Dayanand Saraswati (1824-83), who founded the Arya Samaj, gave the call "Back to the Vedas", drawing a large section of Hindus away from idol worship and exploitative priests. Arya Samaj established excellent educational institutions and worked to raise the status of the backward classes. It introduced proselytization, which was no part of the Hindu traditions. Arya Samaj opposes idol-worship. The Vedic tradition involved sacred sacrifice in the open. The Indo-Aryans did not build permanent structures for the practice of their religion. Temples began to be built much later when worship and supplication were added to sacrifice in the Hindu religious ethos. Swami Dayanand came from the state of Prime Minister Narendra Modi who had used regional pride as an electoral card. Curiously, videos glorify several sons of Gujarat, but not this Arya Samaj founder! Praising this great Gujarati will be problematic for the party that made the Ram Temple the central issue of its political campaign.

In Bengal, Raja Rammohun Roy (1774-1833) founded the Brahmo Samaj facing opposition by orthodox Hindus who were dead set against his progressive outlook on social matters. He advocated modern education and wanted Indians to learn science and technology. His agitation led to the abolition of the criminal practice of Sati that ordained a wife to commit suicide by plunging into the fire consuming her dead husband. Another new school of Hinduism developed in Bengal under the influence of Ramakrishna Paramhamsa (1834-86) that appealed to the common man who prays before a deity without bothering about theology. This communication with God, known as the Bhakti movement, became very popular. In the late 15th century Bengal, Chaitanya Mahaprabhu mesmerised his followers, leading them in congregational chanting, Sankirtan. There were reformers in south India who are venerated by millions of Hindus. In British India, the conservative Hindu leaders debated with reformers vigorously, but that contestation was due to clashing beliefs and not a political strategy for use in a democracy. Today the orthodox Hindu leaders who are corralled into supporting Prime Minister Modi have no interest in theological debates.

In the current atmosphere, Hindus hesitate to even talk of reforms lest they are called anti-Hindu. Political mobs are unleashed on the few reformists asserting the inclusiveness of Hinduism and fighting bigotry. Swami Agnivesh, a social activist who propagated the Vedic tradition, faced physical assaults. That did not deter him from continuing his struggle against superstitions that defile religion. Swami Agnivesh lamented that politicians promote belief without truth. He reminded the people that the Vedic religion identified God with truth and Gandhi went a step further by saying that "Truth is God".

The Hindu nationalists always opposed religious reforms. In Nehru's secular India, they protested strongly, but the Government went ahead taking steps for improving the status of Hindu women. Today it seems like a miracle that in the face of horrendous Partition-related Hindu-Muslim killings, the Congress leaders managed to establish a secular state. That feat was made possible by Hinduism's spirit of tolerance and mass adoration of the secular leaders. The parent bodies of today's Hindutva forces failed to politically challenge Nehru and destroy the Nehruvian ethos. Nehru had called development projects the new temples of India! The slogan "Hinduism in danger" had no appeal then as Hindus had enough self-confidence. That was the India that was! Since then much water has flowed down the holy Ganga. Hinduism now figures in a story of regression. Read the newspapers, listen to the TV "debates" and see the WhatsApp-trained ignorant armies clash day and night.

Courtesy: *Open Democracy*

Conversion of a Hindu Priest

If religious passions are inflamed, it is election time. Every regular visitor to India knows it. India has just witnessed the rare event of a Hindu priest becoming the Chief Minister of its politically most influential state of Uttar Pradesh. Ajay Singh Bisht became Yogi Adityanath and after the death of his "spiritual father" became the head of his religious establishment. Prime Minister Narendra Modi campaigned hard to win the state assembly elections for his party and then ensured that the state is ruled by a monk in saffron clothes who converts Christians to Hinduism and delivers anti-Muslim speeches.

In the ancient Hindu tradition, the priests preached and the rulers ruled. The division of labour is clearly marked; based on the accident of birth or by the virtue of the person's conduct. The priest enjoyed a status higher than that of the king and was respected by the ruler as his Guru and adviser. But a priest would never be the king.

The ancient Hindu traditions notwithstanding, Yogi Adityanath is following the footsteps of some Hindu priests who began to participate in politics in order to challenge Nehru immediately after the independence. They were upset as Nehru talked to millions of his countrymen about the need to develop a scientific temper and march towards modernity. Nehru was the prime target of the Hindu right wing political formations that attracted many heads of the Hindu religious establishments. Of course, they could not mount a significant challenge during all these decades and no serious setback was caused to the nation's secular ethos.

The new U. P. Chief Minister who transformed himself from an ordinary mortal into a Yogi took to politics like duck to water and has been winning parliamentary elections for years. This priest's fiery speeches and hateful rhetoric promoted the consolidation of the Hindu votes in the 2014 parliamentary elections and the latest state assembly elections. For the same reason, the new Chief Minister has caused unease among those who see this as an initial step in the grand plan for eventually turning India into a majoritarian state, called Hindu Rashtra.

The Yogi's selection also indicates that Prime Minister Modi does not want to take any risk in 2019 when he would seek a second term. He has figured out that he cannot win without the consolidation of the Hindu votes and without a promise to end the appeasement of the Muslims. Some Muslims may vote for him out of fear. His party sent a strong political message when it did not select even one Muslim candidate in the state elections. Modi's devotees have heartily welcomed the selection of the Yogi. One commentator applauded Modi for staging the third disruptive event after the surgical strike against Pakistan and demonetisation.

A Yogi becomes a Commissar! But Hindus pray for a commissar to become a Yogi, a more evolved being. Many Hindus would say that this militant-monk, this fire-brand BJP leader who spreads hate is no Yogi.

If Adityanath looks up the meanings of the Sanskrit words yoga and yogi, he would give up his divisive politics and uphold the principle of unity in diversity. Yoga signifies union, balance and moderation. In New York, "Hot Yoga" is a brand but a true Yogi cannot go about exposing himself to criminal cases and fuelling violence against a community. But all this does not matter because the Prime Minister is behind the Yogi and the media is suffused with comments applauding Modi's astuteness. Before the state's Chief Minister was selected, the Yogi's followers went around shouting the slogan that those who want to live in the state must hail their Yogi! The RSS saw Yogi's potential. This Yogi also runs a Hindu youth organisation, independent of the BJP.

The Hindu card matters in elections but its effectiveness rises and falls from time to time. Even in the recent surcharged sectarian atmosphere, the BJP would not have got such an overwhelming majority had it projected this Hindu monk as the chief ministerial candidate.

In his poll campaign, Modi used the themes of development and Hindutva (Hinduness) in the right proportions. Thus the selection of the monk after winning the election has been described by a commentator as "bait and switch".

Hinduism marks a clear distinction between the spiritual and temporal power. So is an ancient religion transforming contemporary politics or the ruling party's politics modifying Hinduism?

This reporter, steeped in the Hindu tradition, was horrified when first he saw the Knights of Armour glorified in Christian churches or read about a Pope of a bygone era who issued a clarion call for the destruction of the non-Christians. Like the Christian churches of the yore, several Hindu temples and self-appointed Hindu saints are very wealthy, owning large sums of cash, gold and real estate. If Great Britain learns from the largest democracy, the Conservative Party could groom the Vicar of Bray to be the next Prime Minister!

But Yogi's selection upset some of Modi's followers. They were mesmerised by Modi's development dreams. Now they advise Modi to be like Nehru or at least discipline the "foul-mouthed fanatics" in his party. These innocent columnists driven by their hatred of the Congress regime never understand where Modi came from. They ignored Modi playing the religion card during his election campaign in U.P. Modi gathered more votes for his party by saying that the state government should provide equal patronage to the Hindu crematorium and Muslim graveyard. The implied charge of Muslim appeasement against the state government was clear. They say a person charged with inciting sectarian violence and facing criminal cases ought not to have been chosen, especially since Modi had made a lot of noise about decriminalising politics. Modi will dismiss with contempt this tiny section of his devotees displeased with him over the Yogi Adityanath affair. Their newspaper articles cannot shake Modi's self-confidence. Hypothetically, today if Modi were to declare that in 50 days, he would make the sun rise in the west, hordes of his devotees in India, UK and America would hail him through the social media. With appropriate gestures, he might explain how this New India to be transformed by his New Politics would help the poor. Also the New Sun God would stop appeasing the people of the Eastern India, infiltrators into the sacred nation from across the border! Tweets will blame the Congress Governments of the past for obstructing the change in solar trajectory! After all, Modi is no ordinary man. He got a massive mandate by the people of India. In a democracy, that is the end of the argument.

However, since arguments are still allowed in India, a Yogi becoming a ruler may lead to vigorous debate. Some Modi devotees may be looking for a verse in the sacred texts of Hinduism that sanctions the wielding of political power by a Yogi! The Hinduism texts do contain contradictory statements, leaving scope for argumentation. A Vedic hymn questions even the Divine knowing everything. Are Hindus more spiritual than the westerners? Is the concept of monkhood different in Hinduism and Buddhism? If Buddhist monks can turn violent, why can't the Hindu monks do the same? Why do the Jain monks refrain from hurting even the insects in the air and on the ground? Did Gandhi weaken the nation by preaching nonviolence? Isn't muscular Hinduism needed to fight the Islamic fundamentalism, as Yogi Adityanath keeps saying. Hinduism experts have to seek answers to such questions. Political analysts may tell us whether the Yogi was chosen because he belongs to a dominant caste. Could a Hindu priest belonging to the small Brahmin community have been chosen in his place? The academics joining the fray will invite hostile reaction. American scholars of Hinduism are more vulnerable as some recent events have shown. They will be rewarded if they cite a sacred text justifying the Yogi becoming the King! The view that the Hindu tradition marks a distinction between the spiritual and temporal power will be contested through cyber posts and You Tube videos. The Hollywood Hindus have been encouraged by the resurgence of Hindu nationalism in India now ruled by the "Emperor of Hindu Hearts". They run a rapid response team to rubbish any criticism of Modi. Even devout Hindus committed to the nation's secular Constitution are called "sickular" and "fake Hindus".

Someone well-versed in the sacred literature of Hinduism rarely questions the political Hindus. One exception was the late Ramu Gandhi, Mahatma Gandhi's grandson, a teacher of philosophy. After the BJP's movement to build a temple to Lord Ram at a place where Ram was born, Ramu Gandhi said in New Delhi that as per the Hindu tradition, the place where a baby is born is considered "impure" and thus a temple cannot be built there. Ramu Gandhi's argument did not convince the pious Hindus who demolished the mosque that was said to have been built in that place. Years ago, Ramu Gandhi got away with it, today a philosopher would hesitate to challenge a mob!

The Ram Temple issue has been hibernating. With the Yogi as the Chief Minister, the BJP will push it on to the front-burner. Modi has taken off his mask, at least temporarily. In the parliamentary election in 2019, Modi wishes to use the Yogi. So religious polarisation will be a continuing crusade. Every regular visitor to India knows that if religious passions are inflamed, it is election time.

Courtesy: *Open Democracy*

No easy answer to the Muslim Question

When a minority community is mocked, marginalised, and attacked, its liberals cannot even let off the steam. In an elected autocracy, they organise seminars to which not many come or write articles that one newspaper may publish. In the TV talk shows, they are shouted down by the anchor and a fiery opponent. Most of them prefer discretion to valour and keep their heads down.

A few liberal Muslims start singing the tune from the official hymn sheet. They advise common Muslims to have self-restraint. Some blame the earlier secular governments for maltreating their community which makes their oppressors indulge in whataboutry. This conduct entitles them to enter the official "Good" category and get co-opted by the hostile establishment and rewarded with an office.

A desperate intellectual now seeks a remedy that could worsen the disease. Hasan Suroor, a liberal progressive Indian Muslim journalist-author based in London, has written *Unmasking Indian Secularism*, a book suggesting that India should be declared a Hindu nation that guarantees equal status and rights to all communities. The BJP could easily get a couple of

Muslims to write such books to make the idea of the *Hindu Rashtra* a "new normal".

Suroor conjures up a quick solution of "a new Hindu-Muslim deal" to be struck by transplanting the British model of a Christian country with equal rights for all its citizens belonging to different faiths. There, the Queen is the Defender of the Faith, and the House of Lords begins its proceedings with a Christian prayer! Suroor ignores the stark difference between Britain and India in respect of the citizens' sense of identity and attachment to their religion. Britain's Christian majority is happy to see disused churches being sold and converted into temples and mosques! British political parties know that Lord Jesus would not get one extra vote for them. Unlike Lord Ram, he can perform no political miracle. There are no divine players in British politics.

In India, toxic propaganda and polarisation have so impacted the Hindu psyche that bigotry will not come down if India is declared a Hindu nation. The plight of Muslims may even worsen. There is much in the name of a nation.

Suroor is so affected by the utter helplessness of his community experienced personally by him during his visits to India, that he has lost all hope in the so-called secular India. But the path commended by him is a slippery slope. The weaker party should work for the "best alternatives to a negotiated settlement". Defeatist arguments weaken the negotiating strategy of the weak by reducing possibilities rather than expanding them.

Let us assume India is declared *Hindu Rashtra* with the complicity of "good" Muslims. That gesture of goodwill would be taken as that community's defeat. Muslim surrender will weaken the hands of those Hindus who are imbued with Hindu principles and seek a benign and tolerant multicultural state reflecting the absorptive spirit of India. A wave of triumphalism will sweep the nation amid a deafening drumbeat by the Sangh Parivar activists. Their slogan "Ayodhya is only a teaser; the film would follow" will become a victory cry. Nothing prevents the indoctrinated Hindutva activists from asking for more, testing ever shifting goalposts as per the blueprint laid out by Savarkar and Golwalkar, the Hindutva ideologues.

If Suroor's suggestion gets implemented, the Sangh Parivar would have realised its dream that is not shared by most Hindus. Contrary to Suroor's hope, majoritarianism would expand its power and glory. Narendra Modi would have added one more feather in his cap. His narrative thrives on an ever-expanding list of enemies who thwart the great march forward -- minorities, human right activists, the left, liberals, intellectuals, students, farmers, and environmentalists.

Modi's devotees may want him to rule for ever but political marginalisation of Muslims cannot not last. Muslims are a significant minority and a very large section of Hindus feels very discomforted with what is going on. In a democracy, a minority is not as powerless as it is presumed. The Hindu right-wing, a minority, demonstrated that sustained groundwork with missionary zeal in the age of social media can give it transformative power. In America, "a backward, oligarchic, misogynist minority is trampling the rights and the will of the majority" and it can hold the nation to ransom.

In India, the Muslim community can counter political marginalisation by rejecting its devious divisive leaders bought over by the BJP. Indian capitalists may realise that communalism is not good for business. The common man may find that communalism makes him jobless. Experts will point out that communalism is bad for the blossoming of the individual's and nation's potential.

The consequences of the forces unleashed touching ever new constituencies, closer and closer to home, may awaken a larger section of Hindus to the havoc played with their society and nation. This may lead to a moral awakening. The hope lies in some iconic leader calling the bluff and presenting a credible alternative narrative of living and letting live – celebrating life, development, and diversity – promising economic opportunity, freedoms, and dignity.

A saturation point or even a tipping point may reach, causing a political setback to the BJP, making the violent mobs powerless, deprived of help from government officials, police, and lower judiciary. Once the tide turns against the ruling party, the process of auto-correction will start. Civilisational values will assert. Courts, community meetings and inter-faith discourses cannot make much difference. The problem was created by politics and its solution lies in politics. The current toxic eco system must end for the flowering of a pluralistic culture that accords protection and dignity to a minority. Its status and security cannot be secured by any artificial negotiated "deal".

Courtesy: The Wire

RELIGIONS: Guides or Minefields

These are interesting times for scholars of religious studies. "Religious violence" has emerged as a hot topic in diverse disciplines and major religions are in the news all the time. Some interpret growing extremism as religious resurgence. Others see no connection between this 'resurgence' and spirituality or true religiosity. They attribute it to the fear of modernity, fear of losing one's identity and see it as a revolt against secularism. Religion is used as a political instrument of mass mobilisation for fulfilling narrow nationalistic or larger geopolitical aspirations. It is used to cover the greed for more resources and territories or to justify wars in moral terms. It has led to an upsurge of bigotry. Apart from physical violence, rival religious doctrines are being attacked. One is reminded of the early days of Islam when the new religion was called heresy and a propaganda war was unleashed against it long before Christian jihads were launched.

The spurt in religious violence has come when inadequacy of science is making many rational people explore the sphere of faith and belief, not based on any scientific evidence. On the one side, men of different faiths are trying to find a common ground in an exercise that is considered bogus by purists or fundamentalists (not in a pejorative sense) and on the other by those without belief. Writer V. S. Naipaul sees no common ground between two antithetical religions. Some eminent scientists are wondering whether they are missing out something and speculating about science and religion having some common ground. Many new books have come out on this subject in the past few years, after it had been more or less taken for granted, that science had vanquished religion, in the so-called western civilisation. That was a premature declaration of triumph, considering how many doubting Thomases the world of religion has started producing and how many men of science are refusing to disbelieve. In fact, the latest developments in sciences are driving them to have a relook at the Enlightenment model.

And yet, a new trend that is becoming quiet prominent in the wake of religious violence is the general aversion that major religions have started causing to some followers who, at least in thought, are turning away from established religions, if not losing faith. Some trends will play out in a variety of ways, depending on the traditions of a particular society, others may spark major social transformation in specific areas. The believers may say there is no reason to panic. They will recall that the roar of a withdrawing faith had been heard in earlier centuries too. And modernity poses no special challenge in 2002 because it has always been there -- the only difference being what was modern a hundred years ago is not modern today.

The battles are also familiar. Within religions, conservatives and reformists are at war. Liberal theologians trying to counter economic and social injustices, anger traditionalists and keep acrimonious debates going. Islam is being used to justify violence and being condemned for the sins of a section of its followers. Hinduism is sought to be politicised by a vocal and aggressive minority. Many followers of Judaism are questioning Israel's policy towards the Palestinians. Catholic church in America is having to confront the moral failings of its clergy and there is a mini revolt against Rome since church leaders have been slow to respond to the sins of paedophile priests. The arguments against contraception and the ordination of women are being questioned as never before. The mounting challenge to Church's authoritarian excesses is highlighted in an American cartoon showing one angry Bishop telling the other: "The laity wants this! The laity wants that! Who gave them the right to play God?

The appointment of the new Archbishop of Canterbury created some controversy in the 70-million strong Anglican community but in America, some Christians belonging to other denominations were more upset. One nostalgically recalled how King Henry II could dispense with the meddlesome Archbishop of his time, Thomas Beckett. An American commentator said the relationship between church and state in Britain is as tangled as it was 900 years ago. "Murder is no longer on the menu, of course, but the process of choosing the next leader of the Anglican church is the same volatile mix of high politics, low intrigue and spiritual longing."

American observers are not impressed by the deep spirituality of next Archbishop Rowan Williams, his communications skills, his scholarship, his mastery of theology and many languages. That he is a poet, philosopher and linguist hardly matters to them. They feel perturbed by the statements of this outspoken liberal theologian who called the US war in Afghanistan "morally tainted". Even while his name was being considered for the Beckett's once-dangerous post, Rowan Williams had no hesitation in saying that any US-led invasion of Iraq "immoral and illegal". He criticised consumerism, the Walt Disney Corporation, child talent shows and violent computer games, all America's gifts to the world.

The Arab Israeli conflict, once secular in nature, is being seen more and more through the religious prism, and not just by the fundamentalists on the two sides. Outside the geo-political sphere, the Middle East conflict is having an interesting resonance even among American Christians. The Religious Right, vocally pro-Israel, lends its full support to President Bush's Middle East policy. Several prominent evangelical Christians want Bush to be more evenhanded and challenge the view that their community is solidly behind his Middle East policy. They are asking him to move boldly forward so that the legitimate aspirations of the Palestinian people for their own state may be realised.

What is interesting is that the two groups argued their cases in theological terms, invoking "biblical standards of justice". Those favouring a more balanced approach complained that the other side was distorting biblical passages. One pointed out that there was "theological confusion" among the religious Right about some passages in the Bible, which are interpreted as requiring Christians to give unalloyed support to the Jewish state because "it's part of God's plan for history". The spokesman of the group said: "if you take the Old Testament seriously, the prophets, who were pro-Israel, knew God would never bless Israel if it did not do justice, love mercy and walk humbly before God. And bombing little Palestinian kids in order to get one leader... and then claim it was a successful military operation -- that is not doing justice and that is not showing mercy."

The earlier campaign against nuclear arms or for the eradication of poverty always attracted many Christian groups. The success of these groups was very limited but the commitment of the religious groups was not. The influence of Christian ideals on some professions such as nursing has been remarkable. Some scholars have highlighted an inherent conflict between Christianity and capitalism but their voices were marginalised long ago. When religious fervour is allowed to hold sway and where it is restricted or resisted, depends on the powerful sections of society and their interests. Thus away from the spiritual sphere, the interplay between religion and society influences certain trends and produce unique results.

Religions are not born in vacuum, nor do they function in vacuum. Often, they are products of desperation and are shaped by the living conditions. A small region of the world thus managed to be the cradle of three major religions. In many cases, the rites and rituals of the same faith, as adapted to the local conditions, make them quite different from place to place. A religious dividing line is very easy to construct for the creation of a separate identity and inciting hatred against "the other". However, at times, cultural and linguistic differences are so wide that the common glue of a shared religion cannot hold different groups together in the same nation.

Such current social and political trends pose challenges before religious leaders who, notwithstanding the progress of the separation of church and state and the rise of secularism, are having to go even further and further beyond spiritual matters. They are having to mediate between the exclusivists and inclusivists, liberals and conservatives, violent and peaceful factions within their faith and in the inter-faith context. They see economic issues affecting their flocks. They see many forces taking up controversial social and political issues in the name of religion. The Imams have never shunned extra-religious issues and make political comments regularly in the Friday prayers. And when Hinduism is made a big issue in the Gujarat violence, the Shankaracharya of Puri is forced to travel and condemn bigotry, a politically sensitive issue. Also, when things get out of control, the very politicians who use religious fervour to inflame passions start looking at religious leaders to calm things down.

If political leaders misuse religion, it is not just the secularists who protest but also the believers who see their religion being hijacked by a few. Many faithful, unable to see their religion causing havoc and being corrupted, lose faith and walk away. This happened in Ireland. This is feared to be happening among American Catholics. And this explains why some Hindus are beginning to blame their faith and turning away from it. One typical response to the Gujarat carnage was "I am ashamed to call myself a Hindu". This might have surprised the votaries of Hindutva who had raised the slogan: "*Garva se kaho hum Hindu hain*" (Say with pride, we are Hindus). Even otherwise, for several reasons, the crisis of faith haunts different communities. In some countries, the number of disused churches keeps rising. Many religious leaders are having to stoop to the level of TV personalities, become media-savvy and introduce the media age techniques in order to keep the flock interested.

The most disturbing development is the spurt in religious violence. There is a broad division between those who affirm the irenic and conciliatory nature of religions and those who say that religions, especially the Abrahamic ones, scatter mines that keep exploding. Even going beyond these specific religions, some say that religion, historically and intrinsically, is generative of violence. The former try to defend their case by making a distinction between a "true" religion and its perverted form while the latter insist that religious violence in all its many forms must be accounted for as "religious" and not merely wished away as external to some self-proclaimed ideal form of the true nature of religion.

Some scholars focus on the violent legacy of monotheism which scholar Regina M. Schwartz describes as "the curse of Cain". Those who attack Islam pick up some verses to illustrate their point. With regard to the Bible, even more extensive critical literature exists. A connection is sought to be established between the Biblical legacy of monotheism and the past and present ills of the western civilisation: exclusivism, authoritarianism, intolerance, misogyny, ill treatment of minorities, jingoistic nationalism, fundamentalism, patriarchy and, in general, violence towards the Other. Of course, this view is strongly contested by the great majority which sees the Bible's teachings leading from conflict to peace, and from hatred to love.

Regina M. Schwartz, representing the former, bases her thesis on the use of religion for the construction of identities which otherwise remain tentative, arbitrary and artificial. Religion lends an aura of concreteness, timelessness and supernatural authority to an essentially fabricated product. A transcendental authorisation is secured for an imaginative product. "... one way to understand the Biblical stories is to see them engaged in efforts to strengthen the precariousness of collective identity formations. In the Bible, the identity of ancient Israel is shored up with the myth that it is God-given". The author argues that the acts of identity formation are themselves acts of violence and, of course, the "impulse to define, to delimit, and to possess propels violence". And identity based on shared belief in a particular deity requires opposing others who worship "false" gods. In the Indian context, the votaries of Hindutva thus concentrate only on Bhagwan Ram!

To run down another religion is part of the identity formation and consolidation. Currently, Islamic scholars keep fighting a losing battle against those determined to paint their religion as inherently violent. Their opponents cite select verses in the Koran and link these to the abominable conduct of the Islamic terrorists. Some go to the extent of demanding that these be revised! All that is bad is publicised all the time while the minority voices recalling historical events and select trends that show the other face of Islam are muffled. How many Indians, let apart Americans, are being told about Akbar and his conduct as a ruler which makes the religious tolerance of a secular government pale into insignificance?

Even in calmer times, western historians generally overlooked the era in medieval Spain from 750 to 1492 when Muslims, Jews and Christians lived in peace and harmony, jointly promoting a vibrant civilisation and making their region a major intellectual centre of the continent. Their arts, philosophy and science lifted the darkness clouding Europe. The ruling family was Muslim, Arabic was the lingua franca, and Jews and Christians held prominent positions in Muslim government and society. That society transcended religious differences. The grand vazir of Cordoba in the mid-10th century, conducting foreign relations for the caliph, was a Jew. The man who commissioned the first translation of the Koran was a Christian abbot. A converted Jew, under a Christian name, took Arabic scholarship and storytelling to northern Europe. The Ummayyads, coming from the Arabian desert, had a vision of Islam that loved dialogues with other traditions. Their remarkable achievement made some later Muslim historians accuse them of being lesser Muslims for it. That sounds familiar and will not surprise those hearing the criticism of new Indian President A.P.J. Kalam, who wears no beard and can recite the Gita better than many Hindus.

The once-flourishing order in Andalusia was brought to tragic close by the religious orthodoxy and cultural puritanism spurred largely from the outside by

Muslims from North Africa and Christians from northern Europe. Be it in a region, nation or a local community, communal poison is usually injected by outsiders. The Balkans are constantly painted as a cockpit of religious conflicts. It wasn't always so and once there lived different faith groups in harmony, till the outsiders changed the nature of society. But the most detailed account of this can be found only in a fringe publication. The point of recalling all this is to emphasise how necessary it is in the present atmosphere to ignore warnings about "false Gods" which keep coming from the followers of one religion or the other. The warnings are only designed to solidify sectarian identities and cause conflict with the aim of asserting dominance.

Some western scholars are more honest and while assessing the propensity to violence, they make no distinction between Islam and other faiths. They are specially critical of the Abrahamic faith for seeding the earth with mines. Generalisation does not help, even less so in volatile situations in which memories of religious wars are recalled and repeated by leaders of movements and nations. It is not the habit of the Ayatollahs alone. The Sandhurst-trained Gen Pervez Musharraf recalled the past religious wars to justify his siding with Bush in the war against Muslims in Afghanistan. And when Hinduism was used as a rallying cry for those indulging in the Gujarat carnage, Hinduism failed to show its "tolerant" face. The news stories from Northern Ireland or Bosnia or places where abortionists are firebombed in the name of Christian faith are familiar.

While some experiments in "*sarva dharma sambhav*" and religious harmony were eminently successful, religious fervour has historically been channelised for the cause of winning "just" wars and this practice did not end in the medieval period. Nor is its absent in the self-proclaimed secular nations. It came naturally to Bush to conjure up images of evil and the crusades. During the cold war, Christian church as well as Islamic fundamentalism were effectively deployed to undermine the "evil empire" of the Soviet Union. It was found necessary to paint the Soviet Union as "Godless" in order to enlist religious fervour against it. Had the cold war not ended, the "Islamic fundamentalists" would have still been getting a good western press and feted in the White House.

The issue of "religious violence" got highlighted as never before in the light of exploding Twin Towers of New York. Of course, religious hot spots are currently active in many parts of the world, including eastern and western Europe, which saw enough religious violence in ages gone by. The religious overtones of the conflict in the Middle East are prominent. And yet, a section of those belonging to the Judaic faith makes no distinction between the suffering of the Israelis and that of the Palestinians. Similarly, a Palestinian suicide bomber has nothing to do with Osama bin Laden. For that matter, the secular government of Iraq has little in common with the one in Saudi Arabia but they are clubbed together because "faith" is seen as the driving force behind their resistance or opposition.

Islam has been brought into disrepute, with the combined efforts of the terrorists as well as those chasing them. The more it is repeated that the war is not against Islam, the less convincing it sounds to millions in the world. In any case, at least in America, the Christian Right would willingly admit that the war is and ought to be against Islam. An anti-Islamic campaign in America has led to several incidents. A state security official raiding a Muslim home felt like scribbling words against Islam on a faith-themed calendar. It is more than a mere theological conflict. Islam has got sucked into geopolitical games and it cannot extricate itself because it makes no difference between religion and politics. In this age, the image matters. There are enough Muslims who have no problem with wielding the "sword of Islam". Their militancy springs from a religious reservoir and they have a vision about their religion. Of course, they have grievances about political injustice but the agenda goes beyond mere political and economic aims.

In India, when the so-called Hindu nationalists try to imitate Islamic fundamentalists, the vision is primarily political, not religious. Hindu and Islamic extremists may share some common tactics but their sources of discontent are very different. Except the competitive sectarianism, or the use of Toyota vehicle, there is nothing common between the Hindutva elements and Islamic extremists. This aspect is not studied and all "fundamentalists" are clubbed together, as if the source of the pain or resentment is the same. One cannot say that the Hindu nationalists are fighting against "modernity" or the invasive influence of the west, or the Great Satan. In fact, they are not. They are quite comfortable with modernity and the western values. They do not lack self-confidence or feel frustrated and do not resent the west in general or America in particular. They see Hinduism merely as an instrument for political mobilisation. they want to use it for polarising society to firm up identities for an endless conflict designed to lead to political and economic dominance of one faith group subscribing to a specific version of Hinduism.

The Islamic militants, on the other hand, feel frustrated by their powerlessness in the face of the western onslaught. They see the west still ruling their countries by proxies. They fear "modernity" and cultural invasion and dilution of the principles of their faith which once had power and influence over "others". And in their religion, the fundamentals allow and encourage their political grievances to be taken up on the religious platform. They have major political and cultural grievances against America. They resent the US support to Israel and the oppression of the people of Palestine. Osama bin Laden specifically opposed the presence of the US troops in his holy land of Saudi Arabia. In many cases, secularism was imposed on them harshly and though the help of an external power and thus a violent revolution followed.

In India, there was no harsh or sudden imposition of secularism because nothing was done to suppress any religious expression and sects bloomed and multiplied. Also, most secular leaders were secular in the sense of not being noncommunal and not secular in the western sense. Many secular leaders were deeply religious. Congress leader Kamalapati Tripathi spent hours in daily prayers but his idols in the home temple were looked after by his Muslim assistant. Successive Prime Ministers visited places of worship. The polytheistic Hinduism was able to accommodate secularism well. Thus there was no real provocation for the so-called Hindutva except in the political sense or sphere.

Till the Babri mosque demolition demonstrated the use of the Hindu card in politics, the Hindutva forces had accepted the fluctuations in their political fortunes within the constraints of the Indian Constitution. The state's failure in Ayodhya and its political rewards raised the aspirations of the Hindutva forces and fuelled their ambition to make Hinduism more "muscular". The headway made by them since then has shocked the secularists and distressed the silent majority of Hindus. Some of them are challenging "Hindutva". The secular forces seem unable to mount an effective challenge because they isolated themselves from the mainstream, building their own castles, cutting of communications with "others". The survival of secularism depends on Hinduism. It also depends on Indian Islam and its refusal, in the old Hindu tradition, to be provoked to join a false battle. Many believe that Hinduism, which is the real target of the "Hindutva" forces, will play a significant part.

A renewed interest in classical learning or in Hinduism as a result of the upheaval will make the rise of "Hindutva" more difficult. As Amartya Sen said after the Ayodhya tragedy, the neglect of classical learning created the vacuum filled by bigotry. Slogan-mongering about Ram Lalla is one thing but the situation changes, if one starts listening to Tulsi or Kabir or the Gita. Hinduism has inherent safeguards against bigotry and intolerance. It represents a theological endorsement of pluralism, diversity and non-belief. The multiplicity of gods, goddesses and paths, its "wise men" holding contradictory views and the emphasis on "dharma" are reassuring. So are the themes of the world being one family and "*sarva dharma sambhav*". It has a proven power to assimilate, resolve contradictions and to provide space to all. The absence of a central church, a single book or the Pope, make it a democratic faith tradition fit for the 21st century.

It is this nebulous form that enabled Hinduism to survive assaults and to benefit from alien influences. Whatever was the nature of the adversary, in the past, the self-confidence of Hindus remained unshaken. Some wore their faith on their sleeves or on their foreheads but millions just believed and no one was able to take that away from them. They changed, adapted, reformed and resolved contradictions with minimum violence. Hinduism, tested by imperialism and colonialism, did not require its followers to shout political slogans based on religion. Some screamed at times but that was in religious ecstasy. Others fell silent but that was in a devotion-inspired trance. This nebulous form also made Hinduism a difficult target as the "Hindutva" brigade is finding out. The brigade, disappointed with the current state of Hinduism, wants to turn free-flowing mercury into a block of zinc. The methods of the Hindutva warriors carry an alien imprint and it is not just the khaki shorts or competitive communalism.

Thinker Ashis Nandy describes "Hindutva" as a minority creed and the "Western imperialism's last frenzied kick at Hinduism". He calls it "an ideology meant for the super-market of global mass culture where all religions are available in their consumable forms, neatly packaged for the buyers". Nandy comments on the attempt to make Hinduism a "monolithic and masculine creed sustaining the ideology of an imperial state". "Pessimistically one could say that Hindutva will be the end of Hinduism in India". But Nandy also puts great faith in Hindutva's geographical limits in India and in the new political and social formations challenging forces and ideologies of dominance. These formations cut across cultures, faiths and state boundaries.

Faith may triumph, but without delivering the results desired by the Hindutva forces. The faithful may credit Hinduism with the resilience to ward off the latest attack from within. Hindus like Ramu Gandhi may assert that an assault on a mosque is an assault on Hinduism, a statement more powerful than the manifesto of a secular political party. As demons haunt, believers with atavistic memories, instinctively know that if a demon is born in a family, his nemesis too may come from the same family.

These are not easy times for those promoting inter-faith dialogue but India has a long tradition which cannot just wither away. This writer's next neighbour in London was a Kerala Syrian Christian priest who had studied Sanskrit in Calcutta under a Pandit. In Washington, while seeking an interview with the Shankaracharya of Puri, one found that six Indian Christians, including priests, were even more keen to see him. During the meeting, the small audience, with shared reverence towards a man of religion, was unconscious of denominational divisions. Most Indians still retain a sense of the sacred. An average Hindu never fails to acknowledge, symbolically and silently, a mosque or a church when he passes by it. Hope lies in India's civilisational strength.

Shav-Vahini Ganga

Parul Khakhar *is well-known in Gujarat's literary circles. Her Gujarati poem Shav-Vahini Ganga of May 11, 2021, about the devastating sight of Covid-19 dead bodies floating in the Ganges went viral and was translated into several languages. Here is English translation by Salil Tripathi. This poem is followed by a satirical sequel.*

Don't worry, be happy, in one voice speak the
corpses
O King, in your Ram-Rajya, we see bodies flow
in the Ganges
O King, the woods are ashes,
No spots remain at crematoria,
O King, there are no carers,
Nor any pall-bearers,
No mourners left
And we are bereft
With our wordless dirges of dysphoria
Libitina enters every home where she dances
and then prances,
O King, in your Ram-Rajya, our bodies flow in
the Ganges
O King, the melting chimney quivers, the virus
has us shaken
O King, our bangles shatter, our heaving chest
lies broken
The city burns as he fiddles, Billa-Ranga thrust
their lances,

O King, in your Ram-Rajya, I see bodies flow in
the Ganges
O King, your attire sparkles as you shine, glow
and blaze.
O King, this city has at last seen your real face.
Show your guts, no ifs and buts,
Come out and shout and say it loud,
"The naked King is lame and weak",
Show me you are no longer meek,
Flames rise high and reach the sky,
the furious city rages;
O King, in your Ram-Rajya,
do you see bodies flow in the Ganges?

Sequel by L K Sharma
A Macabre Dance

Come ye all Indians,
come and dance with us.
In this exotic land,
we breath and laugh,
we sing and dance.
We were brought here
by *Ma Ganga*.
Here it is all *Changa*!

Come ye Indians, rich and poor,
young and old! Come to
this Land of silver and gold.
We are having the promised
Good Times here.
Come and see. Come and see.

The Supreme Being released
us from earthly bondage
and called on *Ganga Maiyya*
to bless our souls.

The Mother came running,
embraced us all, carried us for
miles and miles and deposited us
in this wonderous Hell.
Hell is swell! Hell is swell!
This is the promised place.
The place you dreamt of in 2014.
You hope that India will be it.

You will join us soon or late.
But why do you wait.
You will not miss Him because
every five years, He will visit us.
His commission granted us
postal ballots. An office here entered
our names and finger-printed
us as we were brought
wrapped in white. It has machines
on which we place a finger and
a light flickers and reaches India.

We are in His Kingdom.
His agencies and cells run a

high-tech office.
We send messages from here.
That's all we do.
The broadband speed will be
Tripled soon. We will then
flood India with billions of
message of gratitude to the One
who made us migrate.

As NRIs, we remain in touch
with the Fatherland. At the next
Bharatiya Pravasi Diwas,
we shall be present in spirit.
You want to hang on till the
opening of the Modi Mahal there.
Don't. Come and see
a grander Mahal coming up
here in Hell.

Leader frustrates Lover

No area of life or literature remains unaffected by the populist Leader who has wormed his way into mass psyche. Dreams, romance, love affairs, and personal relationships, all are scuttled by the turbulent political situation. In the New India, poets write on the blood-soaked daily newspaper (Gulzar). Couples are attacked by right-wing vigilantes in public places. In the privacy of a room, a lover is incapacitated as she worries about the repressive regime. The miserable plight of a community distracts her from love for an individual. She is deaf to the call by a Prufrock-like young Indian K. Anand Kak who desperately wants to make love in the time of hate. Night after night in her room, she despairs about the bigotry and violence fuelled by the Leader and resists Kak's cowardly erotic moves. Disappointed Kak resents the Leader's intrusion into his personal life. Feeling hopeless, Kak pleads with her:

Abandon Your Cause
Come to Me

I assure you, like you, I too lament
the state we are in. We are all engaged
in a macabre communal dance,
amusing ourselves to death
amid a deafening din.

But how will we get to love unless
you end your obsession with the nation
and hug me with passion.
You live with India, day and night.
Possessed by the idea of India.
You tell me where India is going. You
take me through the day's depressing
developments. I want to take you in a
rose garden. I talk of us; you talk of
India. I am up against a country.
Your heart beats for a cause, not for me.
Your views on India are very strong,
feeling for me very weak. You feel
anguished about the nation and want
me to feel the same.

You like me. Want to see me every night.
I come without fail. You welcome me
but cannot make up your mind as to how
far can you go! You switch TV channels,
doom-scroll, and chat about the Leader's
irresistible rise and unlikely fall.

You never strike a chirpy note.
Our nights are laden with gloom.
You talk of India, its ills and descent
into hell. You say this is not the India
you had seen or dreamt of. India is
regressing. Going back to the medieval
age. New India is mythological India.

You fear a new *Mahabharat,* a grand
battle within the family.

Masses are fed imagined history and
myths by millions of hired internet
nutters. There is an astounding rise
of unreason. Non-issues dominate
faux debates that publicise the hate
merchants, opening and scratching
healed wounds.

The past is virulent for a nation as for
an individual. The Leader invokes the
past. His army fights over memory and
seeks to avenge a Mughal emperor's
bigotry by indulging in bigotry. It ignores
the depredation by the British rulers.

His vigilantes invoke patriotism to drain
away knowledge from society and damage
universities, centres of liberal democracy.
The deafening chants of nationalism
drown the cries of injustice, poverty
and protests against the Government's
misadventures and dismal performance.

Welcome to the Mumbo Jumbo Nation.
March of modernity stopped. Progress
nullified. Intellect and scientific temper
derided. Dissent suppressed. Dissenters
silenced. The concept of truth obliterated.

The idea of India destroyed. Mendacity
rules. Paranoia and mistrust envelope
us in this communal cauldron bubbling
with hatred. Built by freedom-fighters,
India is being demolished by those who
had kept away from the freedom struggle.

Churchill had forecast who will rule
independent India. Some Indians too
feared that India was not ready for
universal franchise. India got too
much democracy too early. They say
had Britain been a democracy in the
time of Robin Hood, that outlaw
would have been the Prime Minister!

For long independent India was ruled
by those who and whose fathers had
fought for freedom and gone to British
jails. These liberals ignored the threat of
sectarianism. Communal leaders took
advantage of the liberal ethos and spread
their tentacles to destroy secular ethos
and promote their version of Hinduism.

The Hindu right-wing failed to
grab power so long as Indians
remembered the tragedy caused by
religious extremism and polarisation.
The fanatics waited in the wings,
knowing that human memory is short.

India's secular fabric developed holes, giving an opportunity to leaders using cadres to oppress a minority and incite the majority by making it feel besieged. They fight the faith of a frightened minority and fragment society.

They proved that liberal democracy was fragile and could be pushed on the path of terminal retreat. We had taken the idea of India for granted. The bubble in which the liberals lived was small and got punctured easily.

In the Republic of Fear, children are groomed to be vigilantes. The power of rumour to destroy dissenters and institutions and create an ugly society is established. Mass consciousness is poisoned.

Language has been distorted. Words given new meanings. Insidious and invidious confront us. Mobs march waving flags as sticks. Menace the Other, lynch the nation.

We are at war, struck by weapons of mass disinformation. Suffocated by smoke of the digital battlefield. No decaying corpses. Decaying women

and men stare and cry, seeking safety
from deafening digital shelling.

An ancient faith hijacked and turned
into a political weapon. Hindu saints
watched it all. Said nothing to defend
their faith and explain true Hinduism
to those claiming to follow this faith.

You say religious right-wingers and
fake nationalists are ruining India.
Secularism buried under 20 million
paid tweets. People's courts punish
those promoting inter-faith harmony.

As to the Gandhian legacy, an MP
applauds Gandhi's assassin. A woman
in saffron robes enacts the murder of
the Mahatma and praises his killer.
She is hailed by her saffron-dressed
followers. Her video showing a pistol
and flowing blood is liked by many.
Some pray at the Godse Temple!
Such weird scenes are to be seen to
be believed. Video wars are fought
with viral lies and fake news.
Indians now live in Absurdistan.
It has become the new normal.
The Deep State watches and rules.
Fear stalks the infantilized nation.
Officials fall in line. As per orders,

they wreck vengeance on the innocent
to settle scores with the critics of the
Leader. Those asked to commit crimes
for political gains are fully protected
and allowed to go scot-free.

Business leaders and Bollywood stars
turned out to be men of low character.
Big A B or C shake their hips in public
and shake with fear in private. They
seal their lips and look the other way
when their few fearless colleagues are
trolled by vigilantes and threatened by
the despotic Government.

Maha Nayaks masquerade as heroes,
fight the reel villains and sell snake
oil for a fee. Filmmakers make films
to please the Leader.

Order vanished. Laws redundant. Judges
know which side their bread is buttered.
Politicized police have been given a new
charter of duty. State-sponsored vigilantes
wield the weapon of religion. They have
tasted blood. Private armies march
through the night.

Conspiracism has won. Manipulation
is the key to power. We cannot think.
We are drugged. Drunk on hate, we

laugh and kill, kill and laugh and
indulge in mass hysteria.
The itch to be violent has gone virulent.
A riot can be engineered at a moment's
notice. Green fields become killing fields
when visited by women in the morning.
At night, the TV studios become boxing
arenas. The power-drunk anchor jumps
up and down shrieking, striking hands
in the air, demanding drugs, to launch
a million tweets praising his ugly show.
Bear-baiting and public executions gone
out of fashion. Humans enjoy dogfights
among humans. They watch the idiot box
and enrich the channels that spread hate.

Clowns play politicians. Politicians clown.
They fool and amuse to win poll after poll.
Their failure of intent has caused a disaster.
All-consuming polarisation has destroyed
social harmony as well as internal security.

The crapification of the Indian mind is
beyond treatment. A novelist needling
politicians with her luminous prose, is
derided as activist-writer. Let us be
hyphenated at the hips!

Poets and politicians are drawn to
the power of words. Poets use these

to express, wonder and find answers.
Politicians use these to beguile and
mobilise people. Poets say what
others cannot or do not.

Some say poetry is a luxury enjoyed by
the educated middle classes and schools
should not teach poetry because it is
irrelevant. "Poetry, though heavenly
born, consorts with poverty and scorn".
Poetry makes nothing happen! A poet
says so. I say no. Poetry makes things
happen, things that are not seen.

Poetry makes you live, helps you cope
with sorrow. It provides a healing touch.
It is way of trying to come to peace with
the world. This "charming nymph is
neglected and decried". What is worse,
studied as text. You believe "the blood
jet is poetry and there is no stopping it."
As a poet, you sense what is coming
long before it does, as animals sense
a tsunami or an earthquake. So, you
know where India is headed.

A culture war precedes a religious war.
It will take decades to recover what we
lost in a few years. Our civilization is
losing its resilience. The genie is out. It
can't be pushed back into the bottle.

The lie outlasts the liar. The toxic
political culture will not let a sensible
leader emerge. No one will be able
to make this country governable.
Future looks grim. Post-truth politics
has ushered in a pre-fascism phase.
and fascism has had a good trial run.
I call India Prozac Nation and get
away with it since semi-literate
nationalists think it is a compliment.
India turned upside down. Bigotry,
misogyny, sectarianism, hatred and
violence have become all pervasive.

You believe protest poems will make
a difference, change the world. Words
are weapons but the Pope has few
battalions and the Leader knows it.
Writers have been maligned
and marginalized. Logicians have
no role. A semiotician in India has to
look both sides before crossing a road.
A philosopher bolts back on seeing a
mob on the street.

Intellectuals who alert the nation
have been rendered toothless. In
future, books will appear with titles
such as *The not so Strange Death
of the Liberal India.*

Conflict has paid a rich political
dividend. Those who engineered
a moral panic will keep the conflict
running in order to demonise the
Other. The people do not flock to
a Messiah during peaceful, normal
times. Perennial conflict is needed
to keep the Leader in power.

You are not a born poet. This cruel,
Violent, divided and fearful nation
turned you into a poet. You enrich
your poems with politics. I see you
writing *Notes from a Dead Nation.*
You smell evil. Recite Second Coming.
"Things fall apart; the centre cannot
hold. The best lack all conviction while
the worst are full of passionate intensity. "

Things have indeed fallen apart.
The beast that was to come,
arrived and we welcomed it!

Your protest poems, infused with
lyrical anguish, boil with rage.
Political is personal and personal
is political. I say the same to those
asking me not to take it personally
and not let my blood boil.

You light a candle, but no light can
dispel this darkness. That Yellow Fog

was benign. The mental fog is dense.
All have been hit by organised rage.
You and I remain on the same page.

Contrary to the mantra recited often,
our sacred *Janani Janmabhoomi,*
the motherland, is no Heaven. It has
turned into Hell that many of its sons
leave and many more want to leave.

Abandon your cause. Please shift your
focus from national affairs to our affair.
Forget Him, think of me
In this darkness, you spot the
Divider-in-Chief who injects the daily dose
of hateful rhetoric, fear and insecurity.
As a teller of lies and super-spreader
of hate, he competes with Trump.

He sells hyper-nationalism that fuels
bigotry, hatred and violence. Comes
from the same state that produced
the Great Unifier. Ironic!

He imitates Vivekanand and Tagore
with make-up and sartorial props.
His stylist will get a national award.

He shows off hyper-masculinity, like
the British rulers who got themselves
photographed with a dead tiger under

their feet. He boasts of his chest size
and carries on his decivilizing mission.

Efforts to legislate minds and control
thought have succeeded. While the
crude barriers to the movement of
protestors are seen by the world, the
ban on the movement of ideas gets
less attention.

Voters like his display of masculinity
and posturing. They go sleepwalking to
the polling booths under the influence
the witches' brew of fear and hope.
We get the leaders we get.

The finely attired Leader struts on the
world stage. Builds tall iron and stone
pillars of identity and turns them into
sites for exhibition of nationalism and
tourism. He wants to be remembered
through grand monuments.

A mass psychologist, who interviewed
the Leader several years ago, said he
had met a text-book fascist. Scholars
are not read. So, the Leader climbed
the power ladder and rose to the top,
fulfilling his life's ambition.

The academic later warned that one entire generation of Indians will have to pay the price for the havoc being caused by the political adventure kick-started through polarisation.

Moderation and restraint are banished from discourse. Patience for nuance is lost. Hope is derived from rumours.

Scholars calculate the human costs of tragic transformation that historians will record years from now. Books will appear on the descent of the nation and the spell of mass hysteria that enfeebled India and Indians.

The scholar who alerted the nation has met Indians to whom India feels like a foreign country. Constant social strife is ruining their mental health. Their pain is proportionate to the elation felt by the vigilantes going after their victims.

You say the Leader intensifies our anxieties and weaponises these against us. A health expert says the endemic continuous traumatic stress will cause a mental health crisis. Fear aggravates the malady.

GDP-obsessed economists pooh-pooh
the idea of the Gross National Happiness.
Some political scientists dare to say that
democracy cannot survive the loss of a
sense of identity and purpose.

Any internal security expert will tell you
that powerlessness increases depression
and makes people more vulnerable
to extremism and prone to it.

Psephologists write on two narratives
going on in this divided nation, one
backed by populism, rhetoric, lies and
state power. The other backed by facts
and reason, rendered ineffective by a
vicious campaign against "intellectuals".

The talented Leader manipulates mass
behaviour. Through dramatic gestures
and words, he makes people angry or
ecstatic, as per his requirement of the
moment. A blatant persuader. He has
gauged our stupidity and pliability.

He may not have gone to a university
but understands mass psychology and
India's religious and social fault lines
better than academics. He thinks big
and has global ambitions. The religious
card has got him a large following of

long-distant nationalists and the
Hollywood Hindus.

The Leader is a 21st century man even
though he learnt to wear trousers late.
His wardrobe is the envy of film stars.
He owned a digital camera before it
was invented and knows all about
camera angles. His mentor calls him
the best event manager.

He understands data science better
than any IITian. He is smarter than
an algorithm in tracking our hopes
and fears. The toolkit containing the
two lets him control the hearts and
minds as he plays the right notes.

His ability to invent false narratives
makes him a literary genius. He tells
tales to conquer the soul of the nation.
Just as the British did with stories of
their supposed sense of justice and
fair play!

He uses simple messages to bewitch
simple people. Rhymes to entertain
the masses. Uses innuendo to say the
unsayable. Delivers his message
without risking legal action. He

commands and controls social media
that gets users addicted to lies.

In conjuring up enemies of the nation,
he gave lessons to Trump. He demonizes
the Other and reaps political dividends.
Unleashes divisive politics, branding
half the people as enemies. Polarisation
divides all but pays him richly.

He came to power by appealing to the
worst instincts of voters and expands
his empire by turbocharging these.
The bigots feel empowered to act.

The mantra of *beg, borrow and steal*
lets him enlarge his constituency. He
wins some opponents by offering pelf
and power and some by threatening to
fix them. He says in public: "I have
everyone's birth-chart", which forces
others to flock to him out of fear. Once
in his party, their crimes are forgotten.

You say he seduced India by envy and
hate and pushed it into the infamous
company of failing democracies.

Corralled a corrupt populace, lapdog
media and obliging oligarchs who keep

him aloft. He returns the favour and
enriches his selected cronies.

The Leader parrots the Sanskrit saying
"the world is one family" but makes
each community see itself as different
from the Other and the Other as the
Other.

He makes us believe the world is illusory.
Nothing is as shown, and everything is
the opposite of what we are told. He
convinces the multitude that facts are
fiction and lies are truthful.

Ignorance is a virtue. Deception is
state policy. We have entered the
Age of Humbug and Hypocrisy.
A smart operator propped up by
bots rules our *Andher Nagri.*

You say the Leader is lucky since the
Big Power has turned Islamophobic.
It is no longer keen to destabilise
India which it used to be during the
times of Nehru and Indira.

The Big Power now sees India as an
ally needed to counter China. It
applauds the Leader for his
majoritarianism. The Western press,

taking the cue from America, used to
run down India and never report
its achievements. It turned friendly
when American foreign policy changed
and the US corporations began to see
India as an opportunity.

Democracy is dead. Leader is elected
again and again in mobocracy. Mobs
approve of kleptocracy and crony capitalism.

A demagogue kills democracy with
ease starving it of secularism.
Communal hatred keeps him in power.
Capitalists nourish him. Eminent persons
want to enjoy his patronage. The poor
hope he will give the promised gifts.
The megalomaniac's writ runs and runs.

Tragedies will be written on repression
used to control distress when the Leader
failed to manufacture consent. Studies
will appear on the dangerous power
of crowds and mass emotions.

These will explain the outbreak of
tribalism and analyse how and why
people came under great pressure to
take political sides and see things in
terms of black and white.

In all this you are right, but I alert you.
You are a single woman. They will
trace you and chase you.

Don't talk about him. Never sing songs
against him or for democracy. Erase
from your mind the words freedom
and civil liberties.

Do not think. Thinking is banned for
reasons of national security. And even
after you stop thinking, be vigilant.
You will be damned because of your
region, religion, caste, or diet.

Don't phone any friend to express
anger about the wretched state of
the nation. Walls have ears. Walls
have eyes to read your thoughts and
transmitters that send your sound bites
to the Agency.

Beware! the IT Cell is watching you.
It has listed you as an anti-national
involved in an international conspiracy
to spread rumors of rapes to defame
India. It magnifies the demand that you
leave India and go away to Pakistan.

You are vulnerable, not being one of
His Maidens who hailed Him and
secured rewards and personal safety.

India is no place for you. Your poems
have attracted the attention of the cyber
goons. You cannot escape the clutches
of the ghoulish machine of the IT Cell.

My messages to you will be published
to portray you as a fallen woman.
Pouted lips on photoshopped face will
go viral projecting you as a pouncing
vixen.

Your photos will be morphed to retail
your "ignoble" past. This is the least
you must expect, if not an attack on
the street or raids by official agencies.

They have finished Gauri Lankesh
and other rationalists. India is no
place for non-believers. If you want to
live in India, you must believe in Him.

You must stop shouting political
slogans in order to protect your sanity
and self. I fear for you. India
is not what it was. Nor are its police
or courts. Bollywood and advertising
industry are held to ransom by
His devotees.

Literature can critique and condemn
the powerful. Not to talk of Orwell
and Auden; Shakespeare, Milton,

Wordsworth, Byron, and Shelley, all
wrote on politics. Dante even paid
for it. Shelley was not allowed to visit
India because of his political views.

You, I and million others know
who is responsible for the state India
is in. He needed no Constitutional clause to
impose Emergency and silence the people.

You feel so disturbed by what
he does to India that you even use
the four-letter word that I cannot
repeat before you.

I detest him for what he does to us.
He has no health warning inscribed
on his forehead. His noise ruins our
love life. He robs me of your time.

He hijacks you to the world of pain
and away from me. Because of him,
you sing no love lyric to me.
You shed tears not for me but for the
nation. But for the dreadful thoughts
about him, your lips would feel mine!

* * *

You ask me how we can keep gazing at
each other and avoid looking at India.
I do feel guilty for feeling romantic and
being in your room instead of the war
trench dug in every house where families

fight at dining tables over a politician,
the elephant in the room.

The reality of India that disturbs you will
kill my romance. I live an anomalous
co-existence, night after night.

Come with me and be my activist-lover!
Not a common tribe. Considering what
we are going through, it is fine. As a
lover in India of 2021, you are who you
ought to be. I understand but resent it.

I go apocalyptic on hearing you. I share
you anxiety. But I banish all thoughts
that are not about us. I think of only you.
Nation is too big and abstract for me.

It is seen differently by different groups.
Some see it in Gandhi's spinning wheel.
Others in a postal stamp. Bigots call it
Hindu Nation, cleansed of the Other.

Fanatics see it as saffron or green. Chefs
call it Turmeric Nation. Real estate goons
see India as a project site with forests to
be cleared and ponds filled up with rubble.
They see India as the next Las Vegas.

Our motto *Truth Alone Triumphs* is
what India should be about but is not.
Tagore warned us against nationalism.

Like Gandhi, he gets trolled by Hindu
nationalists. Patriotism is the last refuge
of scoundrels. They attack the nation
in the name of nation. Their nation is
a map on paper, a figure of imagination
that they invoke to beat the Other.

They paint the nation as Goddess and
masquerade as her worshippers in order
to mobilise fools and win polls.
Their Mother India is fierce. She kills to
protect her devotees. A film imagines a
different Mother India played by Nargis
who ploughs the field to nourish her family.
She bears the burden with courage and
fortitude. She is just and fair.

A poet sees Mother India as a poor frail
woman with dry and dishevelled hair and
a sad sickly face, unable to feed or protect
her sons and daughters. The poet is called
names by the so-called nationalists.

* * *

These images do not matter. Unlike you,
I am not obsessed with nation. I try
hard not to care what state India is in.
I do see the fascists and barbarians at
the gates. I repeat your sentences about
the current situation. But I focus on you.

I wish you will do the same and are for
me, not for the nation.

There are sorrows other than India.
I have no sorrow other than love.
You are more precious than India.
What is India to me? You are
everything. My sweetheart comes
before the mother.

They say if the nation is in such deep
distress, how do I sing a Love Song.
They should know the most famous
Love Song was published during the
War. There is a crisis now but there
was a far bigger crisis then.

Pain intensifies my love. Share my pain
to lessen it. Stop thinking. Feel me all over.
Here, here, and here! I do not want an
anguished citizen wailing about the nation.
I want a woman to hold. Recite your poem,
if you prefer that to kissing me. I will listen
to you on our dismal state and devious rulers.

How long will do that and not what
the couples on the Marine Drive
do every evening? You hear music in
light and see light in music. So, surely,
you must see above my spindly legs and
below my balding head. I hope one night

you would want more than my ears.

One night, when your mind gets tired
and heart gets hot, you will shut your
eyes and see me. That night, India
would cease to matter. You will turn
to me, touch me and grab my all.

On that blessed night, you would feel
the whole of me and I would feel the
real you. On that holy night, you
will discover joy that you have never
known in your life that remained
satiated with ideas and starved of
emotions.

What a real joy it will be to
be going all the way with you. I have
been wanting to go, and waiting to go
to that blissful heaven!

Excerpted from *The Love Song of K. Anand Kak*

L K SHARMA